D1505817

HOLLYWOOD:
The First Hundred Years

by
Bruce T. Torrence

NEW YORK ZOETROPE
1982

HOLLYWOOD: The First Hundred Years

Library of Congress Cataloguing in Publication Data:

Torrence, Bruce T.
    Hollywood, the first hundred years.

    Includes index.
    1. Hollywood (Calif.)—History. 2. Moving-
picture industry—California—Hollywood—History.
I. Title.
F869.H74T67 1982   979.4'94   82-6503
ISBN 0-918432-44-8   AACR2
ISBN 0-918432-30-8 (pbk.)

New York Zoetrope
80 East 11th Street
New York 10003
Published with the permission of the Hollywood Chamber of Commerce.
Printed in the United States of America.
First printing: May 1982.
5 4 3 2 1

Contents

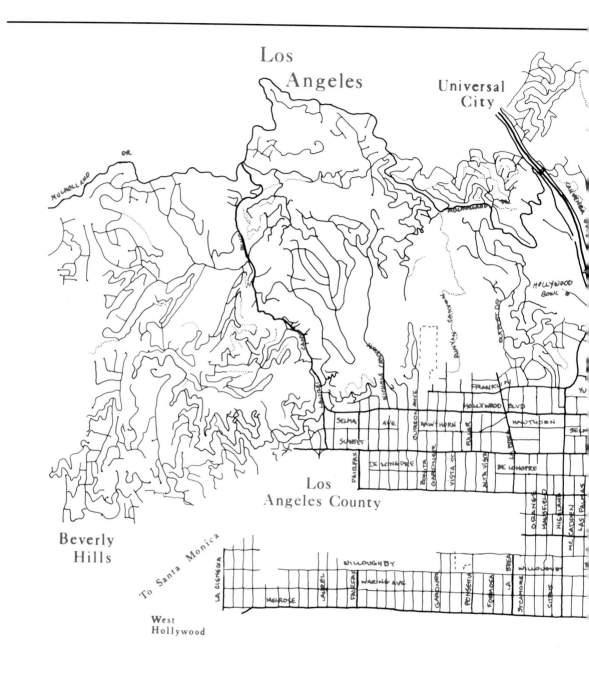

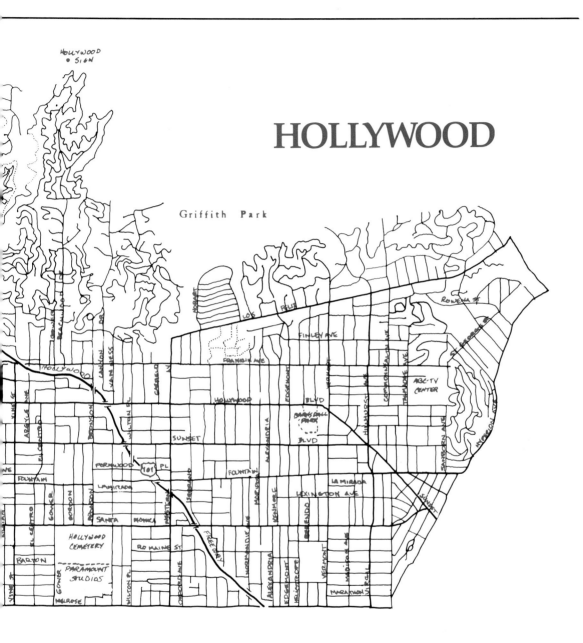

HOLLYWOOD

Griffith Park

HOLLYWOOD
• SIGN

Los Angeles

To my grandfather, C.E. Toberman,
whose love for Hollywood
is surpassed only by my love for him.

Acknowledgements

For their generous and faithful cooperation, the author wishes to sincerely thank all the individuals who helped put this book together, especially his secretaries, Willene Brown and Elizabeth Lee.

Hollywood: The First Hundred Years was set in Palatino by The Type House, Panorama City, California, and printed by R.R. Donnelley & Sons Co. at their Crawfordsville, Indiana plant.

Part One
c. 1879-1918

An Overview

From the Hollywood Hills, 1979:

The curiously flat metropolis stretches across the basin to the Baldwin Hills, seven miles to the south, then edges imperceptively into the remaining 646-square-mile megalopolis of which it is a part. Most of the structures in the panorama rise no higher than the trees that mark its residential neighborhoods, trees that are dwarfed by stately palms that stand in double file along wide avenues. The tall office buildings and condominiums that thrust incongruously from Wilshire and Sunset boulevards are very new and are growing taller and thicker than the palms. Directly below, nestled in the folds of foothills, lies Hollywood: seductress, finger-popping strumpet, Her Highness of Hype, dispensator of silver nitrate dreams, merciless siren, enchanting temptress. Home.

From the Flatlands, 1900:

Hollywood already had its name and a population of about 500 who lived in the beautiful residential community of sparsely scattered two-story homes on wide dirt avenues that skirted the foothills. Tilting gently away to the south was farmland, furrowed under cultivation, and a few copses of trees planted and nurtured to shade the farmyards from the hot, semitropical sun.

To the north, a dirt ribbon of wagon road rose into the crevice of Cahuenga Pass. There wasn't much traffic then, of course, but occasionally one might see a horse-drawn surrey or six-mule wagon or a bicyclist or two. But usually the dust lay undisturbed.

The main body of Hollywood sprawled to the south, down Hollywood Boulevard—then called Prospect Avenue—reclining in accordance with the tract map recorded by Harvey Wilcox in early 1887. And already tall, spacious homes dotted the tract south to Sunset Boulevard. A single track and the overhead electric lines of the Los Angeles Pacific Railroad bisected the center of Hollywood Boulevard.

To the west, one could see the ocean on a clear day. Clear days were more common then, although the same atmospheric conditions that blanket our vistas today existed even then; hazy days were not uncommon. Half a dozen communities lay between Hollywood and the ocean, and, like Hollywood, they were experiencing phenomenal growth, which had begun twenty years earlier and continues still. Hollywood would become a city in three more years, with 700 residents. By 1909, the population would grow to 4,000.

The once-tiny pueblo of Los Angeles could be seen seven miles to the east, across low, rolling hills mottled with citrus trees. It was a city of 100,000 then, and almost daily inched closer to its rendezvous with Hollywood. Already its first high-rise, a nine-story building at Sixth and Main streets, towered in the distance.

Hollywood's residents went about their business on peppertree-shaded dirt streets, bordered by dirt sidewalks and curbs of rocks removed from the fields under cultivation. They paid scant attention to stories that some fellow was making one of those moving pictures—called *The Count of Monte Cristo*—in Los Angeles and on the beach at Santa Monica. None of the farmers, developers, and entrepreneurs who were busy expanding their quiet suburb could imagine that, owing to that moving picture, their town was destined to become one of the most famous place-names in history—a place called Hollywood.

And this is her story.

The Gabrielino Indians are the first recorded residents of what is now Hollywood. They were noted in a diary kept by a priest who accompanied Don Gaspar de Portola and a small party of Spanish explorers on an expedition from Mexico to Monterey in early August of 1769. Portola and his men camped overnight near what is now Elysian Park, and the following day made their way west across the foothill base of the Santa Monica Mountains. The brush was brown from the arid heat and the sparse cottonwood and sycamore trees withered in the blazing sun. The expedition found primitive Indian villages along the river valleys and large settlements of Indian brush huts were found at the mouths of canyons that channeled the winter's water from the hills. The largest *rancheria* [village] was located near the mouth of a canyon at the north end of what is now Sycamore Avenue.

The name *Gabrielino* was given to the Indians by the Spanish, who named them after the Mission San Gabriel Archangel. Although located a considerable distance to the east, the San Gabriel Mission was charged with the Indians' spiritual and temporal well-being. The Gabrielinos, however, have vanished, leaving little trace in history. They left behind only the name by which they knew their land of rolling hills, deep canyons, and gentle slopes: *Cahuengna,* meaning little hills. The Spanish simplified the name to *Cahuenga.* The main passage through the hills to the valley beyond was located immediately east of the Gabrielinos' village and was known as Cahuenga Pass.

During the early years, Cahuenga Pass [*El Portozuelo,* to use its early Spanish name], was covered with a species of cactus known as nopal, and grown as food for the *cochineal,* an insect used in the manufacture of dyes. This area of the nopal was known by the Spaniards as *Nopalera.* After Los Angeles was established as a pueblo in 1781, the pass became a branch of *El Camino Real de Rey,* the principal passageway up the coast. The route through Cahuenga Pass was at first merely a crude, winding trail over which cattle and sheep were driven to and from San Fernando. Eventually it became a wagon road, then a paved highway and, in 1954, the Hollywood Freeway.

Canvas-covered freight wagons from Los Angeles used the pass on the way to Owens Lake and the Panamint Mines in Inyo County. They left the pueblo in the morning and crossed the hills behind Hollywood during the first day's travel, then spent the night by a river near what is now Universal City. The following morning the mules were doubled up to cross the river. The next night was spent at the San Fernando Mission, which was a hard day's travel in the deep sand of the San Fernando Valley. It wasn't until the 1870s that the first oasis wayside inn was built on the long road north, an unpainted two-story wooden toll station known as the Pass Hotel or Eight-Mile House.

Kit Carson was among the carriers who used the Cahuenga Pass to deliver the overland mail from the United States to Monterey. The first mail arrived in Los Angeles in May 1848. Ten years later John Butterfield had the mail-carrying contract. His famous stages took twenty-three days from St. Louis to San Francisco through the Cahuenga Pass.

The pass was the site of a number of minor skirmishes that nonetheless were significant in California history. War was declared in 1846 between the United States and Mexico, whose weak government controlled California. General Andres Pico surrendered to the United States within a year, signing the Treaty of Cahuenga on January 13, 1847, at the *Casa de Adobe de Cahuenga,* Senora Maria Jesus de Feliz's small, tile-roofed adobe house at the north end of Cahuenga Pass on the present site of Universal City. The Treaty of Peace was signed between the two countries the following year, and California became a U.S. Territory.

Rancho La Brea

The Spanish and Mexican governments offered settlers large tracts of unoccupied land at no charge in an effort to encourage colonization of the land acquired throughout the 1870s. A successful petitioner could obtain as many as 44,000 acres. Exact boundaries were considered unimportant, and few owners knew where their land began or where it ended. Maps accompanying the petitions were simple sketches showing any important natural landmark that might serve to identify the land.

The westerly half of what is now Hollywood was part of *Rancho La Brea,* Spanish for The Tar Ranch. The rancho was named for the swamps of tar first noted by Portola's 1769 Spanish expedition. The Gabrielino Indians probably burned the tar for fuel. Later, settlers hauled it in oxcarts from the swamps and used it for waterproofing the roofs of adobe houses. Rancho La Brea was granted to

Antonio Jose Rocha and Nemisio Dominguez, but neither resident of the Los Angeles pueblo ever lived on the rancho. The first permanent resident of the rancho was James Thompson, later a Los Angeles County sheriff. Thompson obtained a five-year lease on half of the rancho in 1852 and built an adobe house and corrals in its northwest quarter. The house still stands in the middle of Farmers Market at Fairfax and Third.

After numerous title transfers, the rancho eventually ended up in the hands of John and Henry Hancock, and John's portion became a large part of West Hollywood. Henry and his wife, Ida, built a small frame house on their portion in a grove of eucalyptus, pepper and palm trees near the tar beds, and Henry began developing the de-

Above: An 1884 photo of the Jacob Miller Ranch near the entrance to Nichols Canyon; the house was located at what is today Hollywood Boulevard and Ogden Drive. At right: pupils of the Cahuenga Township School at Normandy and Beverly boulevards; photo, 1880.

posits commercially. A refinery, which he built to prepare the tar for local marketing and for shipment to San Francisco, operated until 1887, producing five tons of asphalt daily for nearly seventeen years. Workers at the beds commonly came across bones and teeth of saber-toothed cats, wolves, and sloths. It wasn't until the early 1900s that the tar beds became archaeologically important. Henry's son, G. Allan Hancock, gave Los Angeles County the exclusive right to excavate, and, in 1915 he donated to the county the twenty-three acres upon which the fossil beds lay. Thousands of specimens—many dating back millions of years to the Pleistocene Period—have been retrieved from the paleontological gold mine known today as the La Brea Tar Pits.

Oil On Rancho La Brea

Shortly before the turn of the century, oil exploration was on the increase in Los Angeles. Ida Hancock, the wife of the late Henry Hancock, had been approached with numerous offers to lease large portions of her holdings, but declined because of the unwillingness of the petitioners to agree to her terms, observing that unless these were acceded to, she would wait until such time when she could develop the oil herself.

Finally, in October 1885, Mrs. Hancock entered into her first agreement for oil drilling, with Messrs. Lyman Stewart, Dan McFarland, and Wallace L. Hardison. She stipulated one-eighth royalty, reserved agricultural rights and the privilege of continuing to mine the brea [tar], which was still her chief source of income. The first well was drilled to a depth of 1,780 feet, and proved to be a dry hole. Three other holes were drilled, only one of which produced oil in a moderate flow. These operations, however, marked the beginning of the present Union Oil Company of California. Mrs. Hancock signed a second lease with the Salt Lake Company fifteen years later, and by 1910, nearly 250 wells were producing over 3,800,000 barrels a year.

Meanwhile, a man named Arthur Gilmore

had purchased a relatively small plot of land within the rancho and had established a dairy farm on it. In 1903, while drilling for water, Gilmore struck oil. One rich well after another was brought in on his old farm, changing it into an oil field studded with derricks and processing plants and a shack town to supply workers' needs. Gilmore sold his dairy and established the A.F. Gilmore Oil Company, which his son, Earl, developed into the largest independent oil business on the West Coast. This property today is the site of the Farmers Market and CBS Television City. Gilmore Field and Gilmore Stadium, built in the 1930s, have gone the way of the oil fields.

Watching the increased oil development on the rancho, Mrs. Hancock's son, G. Allan Hancock, became interested in learning about this fascinating new business. By 1900, at the age of twenty-five, he had taken a job with the Salt Lake Company. Thus began his three-year study of every phase of the industry, from running gas engines for pumps and handling the oil for delivery, to watching the drilling shafts and increasing his knowledge of geology.

After his employment with the Salt Lake Company, Allan went to his mother to unfold his plans for oil exploration. After careful consideration, she agreed to finance him up to $10,000. He started drilling and by February 1907 he had a producing well yielding an average of 200 to 300 barrels a day. This was the beginning of Allan's La Brea Oil Company, which, during its operation, drilled a total of seventy-one wells.

With her bank account showing a respectable balance, Mrs. Ida Hancock began enjoying the comforts of life that she so richly earned. She built a large Renaissance-style mansion at the corner of Wilshire Boulevard and Vermont Avenue, which she filled with antiques and art treasures she had acquired during her recent travels to Europe.

More than a quarter of a century after Major Hancock's death, Ida Hancock married the Honorable Erskine Mayo Ross, presiding judge of the U.S. Circuit Court of Southern California. With the active management of her holdings turned

Top: The Cahuenga Valley Railroad cut through the heart of the city; this 1893 photo was taken at the corner of Hollywood and Wilcox; residents complained that "the engines caused great noise and frightened horses." Bottom: An 1895 panorama of Hollywood, looking south from what is now Barnsdall Park.

over to her son, Allan, she was able to pursue her travels and charitable endeavors without restriction. After a short illness, she passed away March 15, 1913, in her seventieth year.

Rancho Los Feliz

When the *Pueblo de la Nuestra Senora la Reina de Los Angeles* was founded in 1781, someone was needed to keep order. Jose Vincente Feliz, a corporal of the guard at the San Diego presidio, was given special powers and sent north for the task. Feliz was an able administrator, and soon he was named *comisionado* of the fledgling pueblo, an office he held until the end of the century when civil officials took over from the soldiers. Feliz retired from the service of the King of Spain and was issued a grant to *Rancho Los Feliz*, a tract of nearly 7,000 acres, from what is now Gower Street on the west, to the Los Angeles River on the east, and from the top of the hills on the north, to the Los Angeles pueblo limits on the south.

Rancho Los Feliz was situated in an ideal location, just a few miles from the pueblo's plaza, with a road to Santa Barbara crossing its southwest corner. Its fertile soil and abundant water made the land superior for agriculture and cattle raising. Maria Ygnacia, the wife of one of Feliz's sons, inherited the rancho when Feliz died. She later married Juan Diego Verdugo, but the rancho remained the property of her and her children, who sold their portion for a dollar an acre when Señora Feliz died in 1861.

The rancho went through many owners for the next twenty years, until a large portion came into the hands of Griffith J. Griffith in 1882. Parts of the rancho to the west and south became fine residential sections under Griffith's ownership, but thousands of acres remained wilderness. Griffith offered 3,015 wilderness acres to the city of Los Angeles in 1896 as a gesture of gratitude for his prosperity. The acreage was to be used as a public park, now known as Griffith Park. City officials accepted the deed two years later. The Greek Theatre was built in the park in 1930 and the Grif-

Top: A panoramic view of Hollywood [1896], looking south from Laughlin Park, which later became Los Feliz Heights. Opposite page: Travelers camp near the Cahuenga Pass; photograph, 1892.

fith Park Observatory opened to the public in 1935.

Growth and Development

The U.S. Congress passed a law in 1851 requiring confirmation by American authorities of all Spanish or Mexican land grants. But the time allowed was short, and many landowners who did not understand English failed to have their grants confirmed. They lost title to their land, which was acquired eagerly by farmers and developers from the East.

In 1853, after losing his rancho in this manner, Don Tomas Urquidez took up land in the northern part of the Cahuenga Valley and built the first adobe dwelling in Nopalera. His residence was located on the site of an old Indian burial grounds, at what is now the northwest corner of Franklin

Hollywood residents pose in front of the Sackett Hotel at Hollywood and Cahuenga, 1899.

and Sycamore avenues.

The growth continued until a prolonged drought ended it in 1860. Dead or dying cattle littered the Cahuenga Valley, and packs of marauding coyotes prowled the parched ranchos. Discouraged settlers who looked to the sky for a hint of clouds saw only circling buzzards. Growth slowed until late in the decade, when a government surveyor named John Goldsworthy laid out the Cahuenga Valley in 160-acre tracts called quarter sections. Where a section had been granted previously, another section was given to the railroad, and these "lieu" parcels, along with other government land, were put on the market for $1.25 an acre.

The parcels again were grabbed by farmers who had made their way to California from all over the world. Adobe gave way to board-and-batten houses, with side porches, wells, windmills, and gardens. The broad, rolling acres were devoted to the raising of hay and grain.

One of these farmers was John T. Gower, who came *east* to California! Gower and his family migrated to the valley from Hawaii in 1869 and bought a 160-acre plot between Sunset Boulevard and Melrose Avenue, from Bronson to Gower streets. The Gowers purchased mowers, hay rakes, and other machinery and harvested not only their own crops, but those of farmers from as far away as the Redondo and Palos Verdes hills. The Gowers bought additional land and, by 1875, had 400 acres sown in wheat and barley.

The prime farmland in the Cahuenga Valley was slightly to the south of the hills, near what is now Santa Monica Boulevard, known then as the Foothill Road. The land north of Sunset Boulevard

was considered useless for anything but sheep grazing. That land, however, lay in a frostless belt that made possible the raising of subtropical fruits and winter vegetables. The belt runs along the foothills, varying in width from half a mile to a mile and a half, and is almost entirely free from frost even during the coldest winters. The area also has an almost daily fresh, gentle ocean breeze that tempers the heat of summer and the cold of winter. Farmers raised bananas and tropical fruits and, with the help of Chinese labor, grew peas, beans, tomatoes, and peppers.

One of the valley's first farmers was Jacob Miller who, in 1877, purchased one half of a sheep ranch near the foothills east of Laurel Canyon. The land proved to be extremely fertile and abundantly rewarded the efforts of the new owner.

Ten years after the Gowers made the Ca-

Opposite page: The Pass School and its 1896 student body. The school was located on the south side of Sunset Boulevard, just east of Gordon Street. Above: The ranch of Jose Mascarel, near what is now the intersection of Franklin Avenue and Gower.

huenga Valley their home, J.B. Rapp took up forty acres north and south of Franklin Avenue at Beachwood Drive, where he raised pineapples, dates, tomatoes, beans, oranges, lemons, avocados, cherimoyas, and the usual garden vegetables, while continuing his business in the city as a locksmith. Rapp became involved in community affairs in addition to acting as a trustee of the Pass School.

Another pioneer farmer was Dennis Sullivan and his wife, Margaret, who homesteaded a quarter section of land between Melrose Avenue and Sunset Boulevard just west of Vermont Avenue. Horticultural interest prompted him to experiment with fruit-growing and the planting of pepper and eucalyptus trees. In addition to his farming interest,

Sullivan became a prosperous rancher and a champion for the development of the community.

Remi Nadeau, a rich French sheepman who later built the Nadeau Hotel in Los Angeles, grazed his sheep on 1,000 acres, mostly on the Lick Tract, near Los Feliz Boulevard and Edgemont Street. He later disposed of his sheep and began raising grain. He also ran a freight line of twenty-mule teams through the Cahuenga Pass between the rich mines to the north and the railroad terminus in Los Angeles.

Camels and Desperadoes

Stories concerning the human condition in the Cahuenga Valley are myriad and as fascinating as those of any area in the settling of the West. There are adventurous tales of success and failure, frustration and triumph, but all are marked with that characteristic common to American frontiersmen: tenacity. The unsung heroes are the men and women who settled in the Cahuenga Valley, toiled, raised families, and lived quiet, productive lives. One could fill volumes with their stories, but most of them were never recorded. The unusual settlers are the ones whose stories are known; one of the most colorful was a man named George Caralambo, known as Greek George.

Greek George drew considerable attention by arriving in the Cahuenga Valley with a drove of camels. He had purchased them in the Turkish Gulf of Izmir, and had brought them to California as part of a United States War Department experiment to open a wagon road from Fort Defiance, New Mexico, to Fort Tejon, California. But the Civil War interrupted the experiment and it was abandoned. The camels were turned loose and roamed free in what today is Hollywood and in other parts of the Cahuenga Valley. Occasionally, a camel or two would be rounded up and raced against horses in the fiestas at the tiny pueblo at Los Angeles. Apparently the camels didn't multiply in numbers sufficient to survive, and all trace of them was gone by the turn of the century.

Greek George remained in California and be-

Looking south [toward Hollywood] down the Cahuenga Pass in 1889. The Hollywood Freeway follows the same general route.

came a naturalized citizen in 1867, choosing the name George Allen. The adobe home he built near what is now Kings Road and Santa Monica Boulevard was the setting for yet another colorful incident in Cahuenga Valley history: the capture of the notorious bandit Tiburcio Vasquez.

Vasquez was born in Monterey County in 1837. He opened a dance hall and saloon in Monterey at age sixteen, and by age twenty was sent to San Quentin for horse stealing in Los Angeles. He escaped, was recaptured, and served his sentence till 1863. After his release, it became evident that he hadn't been rehabilitated, for he was soon leading a band of desperadoes who, among other unsavory activities, killed three men at *Tres Pinos* and robbed stagecoaches along the Owens River Road.

The bandit wasn't above petty extortion either, and many of the valley's ranchers were pressed into his aid in return for promised immunity from his desperadoes. Eugene Plummer, a man who eventually purchased Greek George's adobe house, was requested to buy ten pairs of boots and to place them in a cave at the head of the canyon west of Cahuenga Pass Road. Plummer did so, and, in return, found in his corral three horses that had been stolen from his ranch the week before.

In 1874, at San Gabriel, Vasquez tied Alexander Reppito to a tree and made him sign an $800 check drawn on Reppito's Workman and Temple Bank. He then sent the victim's young nephew to the bank for the cash, threatening to kill Reppito if the boy failed to return alone with the money.

Shortly after the Reppito caper, Sheriff William R. Howland of Los Angeles learned that Vasquez was a "guest" at the adobe home of Greek George, about two miles southwest of Cahuenga Pass.

At early daylight on May 14, a posse from Los Angeles surrounded Greek George's house. As several men approached the south dining-room door, Greek George's wife opened the door. Seeing the men, she screamed and tried to slam it shut, but the posse burst in just as Vasquez sprang from the table and leaped through the window. Policeman Emil Harris fired at Vasquez, but missed.

Top [1890]: The Cahuenga House—also known as the Blondeau Tavern—located on the northwest corner of Sunset and Gower became the site of Hollywood's first motion picture studio, the Nestor Film Company. Bottom: The Colgrove Store, on the northeast corner of Vine and Santa Monica, housed Colegrove's first post office in 1888. Opposite page: Hollywood's first subdivision tract map was recorded by Harvey H. Wilcox in 1887, and was the first publicly recorded use of the name Hollywood.

At the sound of Harris' shot, George Beers, a reporter for the *San Francisco Chronicle*, stepped onto the path leading along the west side of the house. As Vasquez came flying around the corner, Beers fired, wounding the bandit in the shoulder, while at the same time Police Chief B.F. Hartley gave him a double-barreled charge of buckshot. Vasquez threw up his hands in surrender. Greek George was arrested, too, but later released.

Vasquez was placed in the Los Angeles jail and soon recovered from his wounds. Later he was transferred to San Jose, where he was found guilty of murder and hanged on March 19, 1875.

Hollywood Gets Its Name

A Kansas prohibitionist named Harvey Wilcox came to Los Angeles in 1883, opened a real estate office, and began to buy and subdivide nearby property. In 1886, Wilcox bought a 120-acre tract that ran from Whitley Avenue east on Sunset Boulevard to Gower, north on Gower to Hollywood Boulevard, west to Vine Street, north to Franklin Avenue, west to Whitley and south to Sunset. The purchase price was $150 an acre.

Not long thereafter, Harvey's wife, Daeida, traveled by train to her old home in the East. On the train, Mrs. Wilcox met a woman who described her summer home, which she called Hollywood. The sound of the name so pleased Mrs. Wilcox

that upon her return from the East she christened her Cahuenga Valley ranch with the name.

Harvey Wilcox was a subdivider at heart. He laid out his ranch in a rectangular grid with the points of the compass and lined the streets with pepper trees. A map of his ranch was filed with the county recorder for subdivision purposes on February 1, 1887. The name on the map was, of course, Hollywood.

In 1891, Harvey Wilcox passed away. After her husband's death, Mrs. Wilcox managed her vast real estate holdings with rare judgment, and donated several parcels of land to religious and community organizations. She married Philo Judson Beveridge in 1894, and from this union there

A hunting party near Franklin and Bronson avenues, 1905.

Top: Gen. Moses Sherman, of the Pacific-Electric Railroad, and Los Angeles Sheriff William A. Hammel [in driver's seat] pose in a Mobile Stanhope Steamer; photo 1900. Bottom: The Henry Claussen Ranch, at the entrance to Beachwood Canyon; photograph, 1890.

were four children. She continued, until her death in 1914, to be one of the most influential people in attracting new residents to Hollywood.

The year that the Hollywood tract map was filed, Clarence J. Richards bought several hundred acres near Sunset Boulevard and Gardner Street. He dreamed of building a town of wide, curving boulevards and fine homes, to be called Cahuenga Township. Promoters began proclaiming the virtues of Cahuenga Township nearly a year before the streets were even laid out. Despite daily newspaper ads proclaiming Cahuenga Township to be the model town of California, few lots were sold and fewer deeds issued, and before long the wild mustard and high sunflowers were again supreme. Cahuenga Township lost its name forever and became once more a part of Township 1 South, Range 14 West, a prosaic description that clung to the land until the Crescent Heights tract was developed there nearly twenty years later in 1905.

Not all early real estate developments were doomed to failure. One that met with success was started in the late 1890s, when Homer Laughlin purchased several acres on a hill just east of Western Avenue and north of Franklin Avenue. He developed it into beautiful Laughlin Park, which, with its tropical botanical gardens, became a choice residential subdivision. Years later, Laughlin Park became part of the magnificent Los Feliz residential district.

One of Laughlin Park's first residents was Edmund D. Sturtevant, who devoted his land to the cultivation of tropical water lilies. In his Cahuenga Water Gardens were rare species from South America, Japan, and Egypt. The lotus was his favorite, and it flourished in all sizes and tints. Most impressive to the tourist was his *Victoria regina*, whose pads were so large and firm that they were able to support a child, and were so displayed for visitors.

Another early and successful development was begun in 1893, when Cornelius Cole subdivided his property, naming it Colegrove in honor of his wife, Olive Colegrove. Cole was a former senator and had practiced law in Washington, where he

Top: Mrs. Daeida Hartell Wilcox; owing to a chance meeting on a train trip east, Mrs. Wilcox brought the name Hollywood back to the Cahuenga Valley. Bottom: Harvey Henderson Wilcox filed a tract map that formally registered the name Hollywood.

had represented the claimants to Rancho La Brea when the title dispute had come before the U.S. Supreme Court. He received one-tenth interest in the rancho in payment for his legal services. The Colegrove development was bounded by Sunset and Beverly boulevards between Seward and Gower streets. "Downtown" was Santa Monica and Vine, where a store was built on the northeast corner in 1884. Later a post office was established in the store, to the delight of valley residents who were weary of the seven-mile ride to Los Angeles.

Hollywood was not the only community beginning to grow. There were scores of other towns cropping up, including Morocco, in the heart of present-day Beverly Hills; Sunset, which preceded Westwood Village; and Sherman, now known as West Hollywood.

The Ostrich Farm and Other Railroads

The first railroad to lay track in Hollywood was the Los Angeles Ostrich Farm Railway Company. The line connected Los Angeles with Dr. C.J. Sketchley's Ostrich Farm on the Rancho Los Feliz at what is now Griffith Park. The first train ran September 25, 1887. Work began almost immediately on extensions of the line westward to Santa Monica and northward to Burbank. Both were completed by the end of 1888. The first train reached the Santa Monica Bluffs on Christmas Day.

At about the same time, James McLaughlin incorporated the Cahuenga Valley Railroad, bought Los Angeles' Second Street Railway, and continued its line west to Wilcox Avenue. The line was sold again in 1894, and the new owners planned to extend the tracks to Laurel Canyon. Residents, however, threatened action to prevent it from being built, so the Cahuenga Valley Railroad decided to build first and argue about it later. On a Friday night, after county offices had closed, precluding the possibility of an injunction, a section crew preceding flat cars of ties and rails appeared at the Wilcox Avenue terminus and went to work. By Monday morning the line had passed down Highland

Top [1890]: The Six Mile House, on the northeast corner of Sunset and Gower, was the first wayside inn to those coming to Hollywood through the Cahuenga Pass. Middle: Looking down Hollywood Boulevard from Gower Street [1900]. Bottom: Bicyclists making their way through the Cahuenga Pass.

Avenue to Sunset and was on its way west. During the next week it reached Laurel Canyon. The angry property owners could only stare in frustration at the fait accompli.

General Moses Hazeltine Sherman, a wealthy Phoenix capitalist, arrived in Los Angeles in 1890 and became interested in the primitive electric railway lines running throughout the city. Within weeks, he purchased control of the rickety Pico Street Electric Railway line, Southern California's first railroad system. From this beginning, he built,

Above [1900]: The residence of
E.C. Hurd, located on the
northwest corner of Hollywood
and Wilcox. Left: Hollywood,
looking east from the hills above
Laurel Canyon; the residence in
the foreground is that of
C.F. Harper; photo taken 1900.

over the next five years, a network of electric street railway lines in the city under the name Los Angeles Consolidated Electric Railway Company. The general brought his brother-in-law, Eli P. Clark, into the management as an associate, and gradually an effective working partnership evolved, with Clark as the front man and Sherman as the money man.

On April 11, 1894, Sherman and Clark incorporated the Pasadena and Los Angeles Electric Railway Company, which constructed the first electric interurban line, running between Los Angeles and Pasadena. Within seven months, the partners formed the Pasadena and Pacific Railroad Company for the purpose of acquiring and electrifying the railway lines from Los Angeles to Santa Monica.

Between June 17, 1895 and May 7, 1896, Sherman and Clark acquired several railway companies, including the Cahuenga Valley Railroad Company. The acquisitions proved to be too much, too fast, and on March 23, 1895, Sherman lost control of Los Angeles Consolidated Electric, when bondholders assumed direction of the financially harassed operation. Sherman, however, retained approximately a fifty-percent stock ownership of the company, as well as full control and ownership of the Pasadena and Los Angeles Electric Railway Company and the Pasadena and Pacific Railroad Company.

In the spring of 1896, the Pasadena and Pacific purchased 5.56 acres of land adjoining Santa Monica Boulevard and what is today San Vicente Boulevard in West Hollywood. They proceeded to build a car barn, a steam powerhouse and a shop on the site. The new facility was named "Sherman," after Pasadena and Pacific's head man. Shortly thereafter, they began electrifying and modifying the routes of the newly acquired railway lines.

When a national depression occurred in 1897 and 1898, the Pasadena and Los Angeles line defaulted on its bond payments. After months of futile reorganization, the line was sold by the court on April 27, 1898.

On June 4, 1898, Sherman and Clark incorporated a new company, The Los Angeles-Pacific

Railroad Company, which took over the financially troubled Pasadena and Pacific line. Through several subsequent incorporations and mergers evolved the Los Angeles Pacific Railroad, one of the largest and finest electric interurban systems in the country.

Eight years later, the Southern Pacific Railroad, through its president, E.H. Harriman, came into control of the Los Angeles Pacific Railroad. Although the sale gave more than half of the 150,000 shares of stock to Southern Pacific, Sherman and Clark remained in active control for some time.

Sherman Township

The township of Sherman, though not within the geographical boundaries of Hollywood, deserves mentioning, not only because of its close proximity to Hollywood, but also because it was later renamed West Hollywood.

Shortly after the completion of the previously mentioned Pasadena and Pacific "Sherman" railroad facilities at Santa Monica and San Vicente boulevards, a small railroad town, embracing twelve acres and surrounding the railroad buildings, began to take shape. For many years, Sherman was the operating headquarters for the rail-

Opposite Page, top: The Glen Holly Hotel, on the northeast corner of Yucca and Ivar, as it appeared in 1901. Bottom: Edmund Sturtevant inspecting the water lilies in his garden near Franklin and Western avenues. Below: A 1902 scene of Santa Monica Boulevard, looking west near Western Avenue.

Top: This two-room wood frame bungalow was Hollywood's first police station, located on Cahuenga, just south of Hollywood Boulevard. Bottom: A real estate ad as it appeared in a Los Angeles Newspaper in 1903.

way company. In addition to all repairs on cars and equipment made in the shops, many new cars were built there. As a result, a large number of mechanics of all crafts were required. As the work increased at the railroad facility, so did the number of employees.

For several years, Sherman was totally residential with the exception of the railroad facility and one merchant, L.J. Quint, who, aside from owning Sherman Hall and Store, was the town's first postmaster. Lots during the early development of Sherman sold for as low as $150, with terms of $10 down and $10 per month.

Shortly after the turn of the century, Sherman and the surrounding vicinity began to be recognized by many as an ideal residential district. At the north, the slopes were being purchased as sites for magnificent homes, while business establishments were beginning to be seen on Santa Monica Boulevard. As the number of residents and merchants increased, so did the size of its geographical boundaries, until it began to border on Hollywood in the early 1920s.

Since its founding in 1896, Sherman Township had never been annexed to the City of Los Angeles. Since it was located in the County of Los Angeles, many residents favored joining the city to secure the benefits of municipal water and sewer systems, better street car service, and more adequate fire protection. Others attacked the proposal, primarily on the grounds of increased taxes. On January 29, 1924, a closely contested annexation election was held in the county. Voting produced a slim majority of 814 to 750 against annexation.

Just prior to the 1920s, the name West Hollywood began to be used in addition to the name Sherman. By 1925, the town of Sherman was torn with dissention over the choice of a formal name. The residents were considering changing the name to Beverly Park or East Beverly or West Hollywood or Magnetic Springs. Though it is only speculation, it would appear that a formal name-change election may have been held, for it was at about this time that the name West Hollywood was beginning to be used almost exclusively.

Top: A Hollywood resident stands
in the middle of a sweet
pea field near Sunset and
Curson. At left: The entrance
to Hollywood Cemetery on
Santa Monica, east of Gower;
this photo was taken in 1903.

Commerce In Hollywood

The first market and general merchandise store in Hollywood was started in 1885 by Alfred Watts across the street from the Colegrove Post Office at Santa Monica and Vine. Watts moved his Hollywood Cash Grocery to Sunset and Cahuenga in 1888. He bought the Edgemont Street store and operated both, delivering goods all over the north side of the valley. His delivery man also picked up the mail on his route and mailed it at the Prospect Park Post Office, until the government stopped him from "robbing" the Colegrove Post Office of its patronage.

Hollywood's first meat man was Jacob Muller, who, in 1885, came to Los Angeles, where he represented the Meyer Packing House, covering the Hollywood area with semiweekly deliveries.

In 1893, he bought a home and market site on the north side of Sunset Boulevard at Ivar, where he established the Hollywood Market, which he ran until 1907. He then formed the Hollywood Ice Company, which he sold to Union Ice Company in 1914. The four acres Muller had acquired at the southeast corner of Sunset and Ivar later became the site of the largest automobile superservice station in the world.

Martin Labaig established the Six-Mile House at Sunset and Gower in 1887, selling meals, beer, wines, and liquor. That same year, Horace D. Sackett bought three 65-foot lots at Hollywood and Cahuenga, and opened the second general store and the first hotel in the Cahuenga Valley: The Sackett Hotel, a three-story building that became the overnight and breakfast spot for visitors from the north, as well as a hangout for the valley's bachelors. Mr. & Mrs. Rene Blondeau bought six acres at the northwest corner of Sunset and Gower in 1889 and built The Cahuenga House, also known as the Blondeau Tavern. The tavern would become the home of one of the pioneer film companies [the Nestor Film Company] during the movies' invasion of Hollywood twenty-two years later.

Top: The pavillion at the top of Whitley Heights; Sunday afternoon band concerts were regularly held here. Below: A 1904 ad for the popular Red Car Balloon Route Excursions.

Cooperative Marketing Begins

By 1889, increased demand for vegetables and semitropical fruits in Los Angeles and San Francisco caused the Cahuenga Valley growers to unite and form the Farmers' League of Cahuenga Township. The purpose of the league was to protect its

members from ruinous competition by providing ways for disposing of their crops. A survey showed that there were 291 acres of tomatoes, 102 acres of peas, 82 acres of beans, and 20 acres of chilis in the north section of the valley.

Six years later, in 1895, the valley's lemon growers formed the Cahuenga Valley Lemon Growers' Exchange to operate a packing house where the lemons could be graded for uniform size and quality, and to begin shipments to eastern markets. In 1897, a large packing plant was built at Santa Monica Boulevard and Cahuenga Avenue. The association's name was changed to the Cahuenga Valley Lemon Association, and over the next twenty years, lemons were shipped nationwide under the brand names of Blue Ribbon, Punch Bowl, and Club, and for local consumption under the brand name of Valley.

Early Churches and Schools

Hollywood's first house of worship, the German Methodist Church, was built in 1876 by the Reverend George Shultz, a Methodist, with volun-

Top: A 1904 view of Hollywood from Whitley Heights, looking southwest. Bottom: The Cahuenga Valley Lemon Exchange at the southeast corner of Santa Monica Boulevard & Cahuenga.

teer labor on donated land at Santa Monica Boulevard and Kingsley Drive, two blocks east of the present Hollywood Freeway. The second church society in the Cahuenga Valley was the Hollywood Christian Church, started in 1888 by the Reverend M.L. Yager. By 1891 it had forty-one members. That was the same year that Harvey Wilcox died, and his widow, one of Yager's parishioners, donated to the church a small lot at the corner of Cahuenga and Selma. Three years later a small church that seated 150 was built. As Hollywood grew, the church grew with it, and eventually the present structure was built at Hollywood Boulevard and Gramercy Avenue. Several years later the church formed a union with the Beverly Christian Church and assumed the name of Hollywood-Beverly Christian Church.

Other citizens met a year after the Hollywood Christian Church was founded to form the First Methodist Episcopal Church South, and, in 1890, they built their church at Fairfax and Santa Monica. This was later moved to Cahuenga and Selma, on land given by the ecumenical Mrs. Wilcox, and moved again in 1904 to the southeast corner of Hollywood and Vine.

The Catholic population of the Cahuenga Valley was forced to travel seven miles to attend mass in downtown Los Angeles until 1903, when Blessed Sacrament Church was formed. Services were held in Drouet's Hall at Sunset and Cahuenga, until a church could be built at Hollywood and Cherokee. In 1928, the church and parish school were moved to 6657 Sunset Boulevard.

The closest school to the Cahuenga Valley throughout most of the 1800s was the one-room Cienega School, four miles overland without roads at Pico Boulevard and La Brea Avenue. The Cahuenga School District was formed in 1876, and a schoolhouse was built at the corner of Normandie Avenue and Beverly Boulevard. It, too, had become inadequate by 1881, and the district was divided again to form the Pass School District.

Below: The first section of the famed Hollywood Hotel, on the northwest corner of Hollywood and Highland [1904]; its 'Dining Room of the Stars' was popular with Hollywood's elite.

While a three-room school was under construction on the south side of Sunset near Gordon Street, classes were held in the home of William Beesemyer. They were taught by Mary Gower, daughter of the John and Mary Gower who had arrived from Hawaii twelve years earlier.

The Laurel School District built a one-room schoolhouse in 1886 in West Hollywood, and a year later the Los Feliz School District was organized and a two-room school with a tower was built at the northwest corner of Los Feliz Boulevard and Vermont Avenue. A few years later the student body moved to a new school building at Hollywood Boulevard and New Hampshire Avenue. Following a fire in 1914, which all but destroyed the school, new buildings were constructed. After the earthquake of 1932 rendered the school buildings unsafe, they were torn down and replaced with new modern structures.

The first newspaper in the Cahuenga Valley, the monthly *Cahuenga Suburban,* appeared in April 1895. It was profusely illustrated with photographs and printed on book paper and was owned and edited by Seymour J. Millikin. The *Suburban* ceased publication in 1899 and the following year the weekly *Cahuenga Valley Sentinel* was started by A.A. Bynon and his son, Fred. The name was changed to the *Hollywood Sentinel* within a few months. The *Sentinel* was Hollywood's only newspaper for five years, then several citizens headed by Dr. E.O. Palmer obtained $1,230 in subscriptions from forty-eight residents and began the *Hollywood Citizen,* which appeared on April 2, 1905. The two papers, with a combined circulation of 800, were merged in 1911, with the *Hollywood Citizen* name surviving. The paper was sold later the same year to Harlan G. Palmer.

An Artist Comes To Town

In 1899, French-born Paul DeLongpre arrived in Los Angeles with his wife, Josephine, and three children, Alice, Blanche, and Pauline.

A painter since the age of twelve, DeLongpre had exhibited his oils and watercolors in Paris and

Top: The Methodist Episcopal Church South, on the southeast corner of Hollywood and Vine [1905], is now the site of the Taft Building. Middle: Children strolling down Sunset Boulevard, near Gower [1905]. Bottom: A 1905 view of Hollywood Union High School at Sunset Boulevard and Highland.

New York before making his way west. DeLongpre loved to wander through the suburbs of Los Angeles on a bicycle, searching for floral subjects for his paintings. He often visited Hollywood, where he found congenial French conversation

GLIMPSE OF PAUL DE LONGPRE'S HOME, HOLLYWOOD

At left: A pictorial section of the *Sunday Herald*, 1909. Above: Hastings' Place, at Hollywood Boulevard and Vermont; 1909. Right: The interior of the First National Bank at the northeast corner of Highland and Hollywood Boulevard; 1910.

A Balloon Route Excursion attraction was the stop at the Paul De Longpre residence, where tourists were invited to have their pictures taken and could buy the photos [1905].

with the Blondeau family. Soon he gave an exhibition in Los Angeles, where he met Mrs. Daeida Wilcox Beveridge, to whom he expressed his desire to build a home and studio in the Cahuenga Valley.

In 1901, he bought from Mrs. Beveridge three 65-foot lots facing east on Cahuenga Avenue, north of the corner lot on Prospect Avenue. In 1902, having found his garden too small, he bought the corner lot, too, for $3,000, in lieu of which Mrs. Beveridge accepted three paintings.

Besides his worldwide reputation as a floral artist, DeLongpre was a man of great personal charm and sincerity. His palatial home, studio, and guest house, with their profuse, variegated, perennial floral setting, made his home one of the most prized showplaces in Southern California. His studio always contained fifty or more finished watercolors of flowers. While only a few tourists visited the Cahuenga Valley prior to the turn of the century, now literally thousands flocked each year to see the famous artist and his floral haven.

Beginnings Of Tourism

The forerunner of sightseeing in Hollywood was established in 1900 by Charles M. Pierce, who operated a coach service with which he met tourists at the Hollywood streetcar depot and took them on a guided tour of the area, to the Glen Holly Hotel for lunch, then back to the depot. Pierce later began the Balloon Route Excursions, operated by the Los Angeles Pacific Railroad. The trolley route, when placed on a map, made the outline of a balloon. Eighteen carloads daily operated at the height of its popularity. The streetcars' first stop after leaving the Hill Street Station in Los Angeles was Paul DeLongpre's home. Here the tourist could visit with the world-renowned artist and stroll through his studio and colorful floral gardens. The excursion continued to the Soldiers' Home in Sawtelle, where the passengers' picture

was taken on the dining hall steps. The photographer then rode downtown on a regular car, developed his negative and printed copies of his photo, and got back on another regular car to meet the excursion, where he reboarded and sold his photos. The balloon-route cars then went to Santa Monica, Playa del Rey for a fish dinner, Moonstone Beach in Redondo, to Venice to see the canals, then made a fast run back to Los Angeles via Palms. The Pacific Electric Railroad took over the Los Angeles Pacific in 1911 and assumed management of the Balloon Route Excursions. Pierce, though, remained in the sight-seeing business, using automobiles and finally airplanes.

Subdividers

In 1901, the Los Angeles Pacific Boulevard and Development Company was incorporated. Among the many investors were Harrison Gray Otis, editor of the *Los Angeles Times*, H.J. Whitley, and George W. Hoover.

The company purchased the land north of Prospect Avenue [Hollywood Boulevard] in an area basically between Cahuenga Boulevard and La Brea, and laid out the Hollywood Ocean View Tract. The more level area was graded and the streets, which were much as they remain today, were finished with concrete curbs, water mains, gutters, and sidewalks. Highland Avenue was zoned for business on the west side from 150 feet north of Prospect to Franklin Avenue, and on the east side from 198 feet north of Prospect to Yucca. Prospect Avenue was residential zoning for the length of the tract. There were to be no multiple dwellings, no dwelling could cost less than $3,000, and no liquor was to be sold on the tract.

The site of the first unit of the Hollywood Hotel at the northwest corner of Prospect and Highland avenues was given to Mr. George W. Hoover, while the site on the northeast corner went to the Bank of Hollywood. Mr. Hoover started the hotel immediately. Shortly after the bank was incorporated, a brick building was constructed on the site.

Top: The Immaculate Heart High School, Western and Franklin, during its final days of construction, 1906; the main building had to be torn down in 1973, owing to the damage sustained in the 1971 earthquake. Middle: Built in 1886, the Hollywood Cash Grocery store was located on the northeast corner of Sunset and Cahuenga; photograph, 1905. Bottom: Farmer Dennis Sullivan plowed open fields near what is now the Los Angeles Community College campus on Vermont Avenue; this photo taken in 1905.

The property north of Franklin Avenue just east of Highland Avenue was given to H.J. Whitley to develop into a residential tract. This he did with great success and the development has ever since been called Whitley Heights.

One of the most illustrious residents of this area was the silent screen actor Rudolph Valentino. In 1924, he purchased his Whitley Heights home, located at 6776 Wedgewood Place, where he lived with his second wife, Natacha Rambova.

When the Valentinos moved in, there was

Top: Looking east down Hollywood Boulevard towards Highland; in the foreground are fields of strawberries; at center is the Hollywood Hotel [1905]. Middle: Traveling east down Hollywood Boulevard towards Whitley. At right: The Casa Don Thomas, built in 1853, was the first adobe house in Hollywood, located near Franklin Avenue, just west of Highland.

much work yet to be done in decorating and furnishing the home. The furniture and art treasures they had bought in Europe and New York had to be worked into the house decor or placed in storage. Lavishly decorated "palaces" were becoming commonplace among Hollywood's big stars, and the Valentinos were not to be outdone.

The two-story house was set back about 150

feet from the street and contained eight rooms, including a dining room, living room, two master bedrooms with two baths, a kitchen, butler's pantry, servants' dining room, servants' room with bath, and a laundry room. Beautifully landscaped, the exterior had extensive terracing studded with Italian cypress trees, interesting shrubs and lawns. A high wall, built along the sidewalk line, enclosed the front courtyard and a high wire fence surrounded the entire property.

After living in the house for about a year, Mrs. Valentino wished to move into the more fashionable district of Beverly Hills, where they could be surrounded by the stars of Rudy's caliber. In 1925, they moved out of their Whitley Heights home after purchasing a large Mediterranean-style house that Valentino immediately named "Falcon Lair."

The first forty-room unit of the Hollywood Hotel was completed in February 1903. Construction of an additional 104 rooms continued for the next three years and, in 1907, the hotel was sold to Mira Hershey of the Pennsylvania chocolate family. As the film colony grew during the ensuing years, the hotel became the social center of Holly-

In 1905, two years after Hollywood became a city, this photo was taken from the hills above Orchid Avenue; population 700.

wood. Stars of the silent films romped and romanced in its Dining Room of the Stars.

The hotel register listed such luminaries as Dustin and William Farnum, Douglas Fairbanks, Anita Stewart, Lon Chaney, Pola Negri, Norma Shearer, and scores of others. Rudolph Valentino had to show his marriage license before he could carry his first bride, Jean Acker, to their honeymoon chamber at the hotel. Many of the great silent stars made their home at the hotel and attended the weekly Thursday dances held in the crystal-chandeliered ballroom. Gold stars painted on the ceiling designated celebrities who dined regularly.

Carrie Jacobs Bond wrote her famous song, "The End of a Perfect Day," at the Hollywood Hotel in 1909. The hotel became almost a national shrine when Louella Parsons put film stars on the radio and announced: "This is Louella Parsons, broadcasting from the Hollywood Hotel." Celebrities from all over the country arrived in 1938 to attend a gala party to celebrate the thirty-fifth anniversary of the world-famous hotel, which finally

fell to the wreckers' ball in 1956.

While the Los Angeles Pacific Boulevard Development Company was promoting their development, Mrs. Daeida Wilcox Beveridge was actively building a business center at Prospect and Cahuenga avenues. Thus the village was divided into two ambitious business centers connected by a strip of a half mile of territory through which ran the only common carrier of the town, the streetcar.

On January 8, 1903, several Masons met for the purpose of forming a new Masonic Lodge. The first regular meeting was held on May 1, 1903, at the southwest corner of Sunset and Cahuenga, above Drouet's harness shop and home. It was there that the first initiations took place. During the following year, more suitable quarters were furnished on the west side of Highland Avenue, in the block north of Hollywood Boulevard, in a building known as Masonic Hall, which consisted of an auditorium over two stores. By 1905, the lodge had fifty-seven members. In 1922, a beautiful, classic Masonic Temple was built at 6840

Top: The Sackett Hotel, which was located on the southwest corner of Hollywood and Cahuenga, was built in 1888 and was the first structure built as a hostelry in the Cahuenga Valley. Bottom: Postal employees and other townsmen pose before the post office at Hollywood and Cahuenga [1906].

Hollywood Boulevard facing Orchid Avenue, at a cost of $250,000.

Hollywood Becomes a City

The United States government recognized the existence of Hollywood in November 1897 by establishing a post office in the Sackett Hotel, with Lineaus Matthews as postmaster. Over the next six years the village of Hollywood was faced with three pressing problems that the Cahuenga Valley Improvement Association, organized in 1895, seemed incapable of solving: Hollywood streets were not getting attention in proportion to the tax levied by the county on Hollywood property; a lack of school facilities; and a growing sentiment for prohibition.

The Hollywood Board of Trade was formed in June 1903 to supercede the improvement association, and at the following month's meeting it was suggested that many of the community's problems could be solved by incorporating as a city. Debate was lengthy and heated. The probable cost of city government divided the village, with Harvey Wilcox's widow—now Mrs. Philo Beveridge—and a large following opposed to the idea. A poll showed a majority favoring the plan, though, and in August 1903 a petition was submitted to the Los Angeles Board of Supervisors requesting the incorporation of the City of Hollywood. Sixty-two voters, of an estimated area population of 700, had

Top: The imposing residence of A.G. Bartlett rests on a knoll just above Hollywood Boulevard between Vine and Gower [1906]. Below: An entry in the second annual Tilting Tournament and Floral Parade, which was held on Hollywood Boulevard between Highland and Cahuenga. The tournament was held at parade's end; riders on horseback and carrying fourteen-foot lances were given three chances to spear white harness rings from posts, at three points per ring. Nine points won the tournament; the winner and his chosen partner led the grand march at the ball that evening, which ended in the wee hours.

signed the petition.

The election was held November 14, 1903, at the Pass School. Balloting began at 6:00 A.M. and was brisk until midmorning. Outlying farmers straggled in throughout the rest of the day to cast their ballots until the polls closed at 5:00 P.M. At the count, proponents and opponents eyed each other across the crowded room. The first three bal-

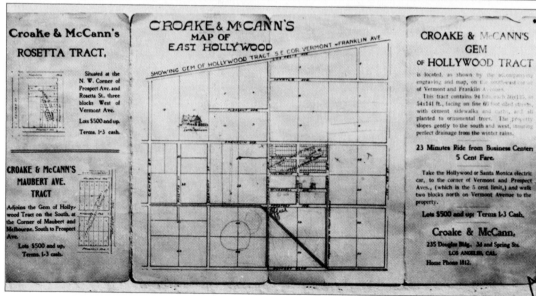

Top: Immaculate Heart High School, shortly after it was built in a mustard field at Western and Franklin in 1906; this Mission-Moorish building had to be razed in 1973 after sustaining irreparable damage during the 1971 earthquake.
Below: A 1908 newspaper ad showing an East Hollywood tract.

Entrants line up on Hollywood Boulevard and await the start of the second annual Tilting Tournament and Floral Parade [1908].

lots were against incorporation. The next was for it, then two more against, and so on until 126 ballots had been counted and the opponents' majority of thirteen was reflected in their happy faces. The 127th ballot was in favor, and from that point on the vote shifted in favor. The final tally showed eighty-eight for incorporation and seventy-seven against.

So Hollywood was a city of the sixth class, with its corporate geographic limits extending from Normandie Avenue on the east, to Fairfax Avenue on the west, and from the top of the Santa Monica Mountains on the north, to DeLongpre and Fountain avenues on the south. After annexation to Los Angeles in 1910, Hollywood retained essentially the same boundaries, but in 1937, for reasons never adequately explained, the Los Angeles City Council passed Ordinance 78,499, officially establishing Hollywood's boundaries as Doheny Drive on the west, the top of the Santa Monica Mountains on the north, the Los Angeles River on the east and Melrose Avenue on the south, a too-generous description shrugged off by many as a typical bureaucratic aberration.

Street numbers came to Hollywood when the Los Angeles Gas Company installed the new city's first gas meters in 1904. Distances between houses were measured by a bicycle with a rag tied around the tire, and, for identification, the houses were given numbers, numbering in four directions from Hollywood and Cahuenga. During the first year of incorporation the eight-member Hollywood Board of Trustees was busy doing as all governments feel they must—passing laws. Immediately enacted were city ordinances creating numerous crimes:

• Prohibiting the sale of liquor except by pharmacists on prescription.

• Prohibiting the riding of bicycles, tricycles, or velocipedes on sidewalks—particularly Mr. Whitley's and Mr. Beveridge's sidewalks, which were the only ones in town at the time.

• Outlawing the driving of horses, cattle, or mules through the streets of Hollywood in bands or herds of more than 200, or more than 2,000 sheep, goats, or hogs, unless accompanied by competent men in charge.

• Prohibiting the use of fireworks between Vine and Highland, and Franklin and Wilson.

• Prohibiting the operation or maintenance of slot machines, card machines, or other mechanical devices in the city of Hollywood, for money or

The Red Car stop at Sunset Boulevard and Laurel Canyon, 1908.

other articles of value, depending on chance or hazard.

• Prohibiting drunkenness, disorderly conduct, and keeping of disorderly houses and prescribing punishment.

• Prohibiting slaughterhouse, glue factory, gas works, soap factory, sanitarium, tannery, smelting works, oil well, or oil refinery within the city of Hollywood; shoddy machines, carpet beating works, laundries, planing mills, lumber yards, factories, or places of business where steam is supplied to machinery within 100 feet of any dwelling, residence, church, or school, or lumber yard or place where steam is applied to machinery within 300 feet of school grounds.

• Billiard rooms, pool rooms, bowling alleys, shooting galleries required to be closed from 11:00 P.M. to 7:00 A.M. and 11:00 P.M. Saturday to 7:00 A.M. Monday. Patrons under twenty-one not permitted. Violation, a misdemeanor, punishable by a fine of $100 or less, or thirty days or less in the county jail.

Arrangements were made with the county to board prisoners in its jail, and on the city hall lot, on the west side of Cahuenga just south of Holly-

wood Boulevard, a 6 x 8 x 10-foot concrete box with barred openings and an iron door was built for overnight detention, but only an occasional drunk ever saw it from the inside.

Three years before Hollywood became a city, the Hollywood Cemetery Association was formed. Against the loud and legal protests of the neighboring property owners, the association purchased a large tract of land at the southeast corner of Gower Street and Santa Monica Boulevard, and there established the Hollywood Cemetery. The first to be buried there was Mrs. T.W. Price, the wife of the village smith. Today this is the final resting place for many of Hollywood's residents and noted celebrities, including Rudolph Valentino.

At about the time of Hollywood's incorporation, the Union Rock Company established a quarry in Brush Canyon, two miles north of Franklin Avenue at the northern end of Bronson. The crushed rock was trucked down Bronson Avenue for use in railroad ballast and street surfaces.

Many Hollywood residents complained vociferously that the trucks tore up the newly paved streets and jarred their homes as they passed in the

night, so a rail line was established that operated during restricted hours of the morning and evening. But by 1918, it had become more economical and practical to haul the rock by truck, so the railroad spur was discontinued.

As a result of complaints from homeowners on Bronson Avenue and of the diminishing need for porphyry, the quarry ceased operation in the late 1920s. The caves, now known as the Bronson Caves, which were carved into the hills by the old quarry, have been and still are used by countless motion picture production companies as location for western, science fiction, and adventure films. To the chagrin of the Bronson Avenue residents, the rock trucks have been replaced by mobile studio trucks and equipment.

More Schools & Churches

The graduates of Cahuenga Valley grammar schools went to Los Angeles High School or Santa Monica High School at their own expense. Holly-

Top: S.H. Laverty stands on the steps of a street car as it emerges from the Hill Street Tunnel on Hollywood's "Tunnel Day"; the completion of this tunnel cut twelve minutes from the time it took to travel from Los Angeles to Hollywood. Bottom: Hollywood businessmen participated in a "Fats vs. Leans" game on the Hollywood High School diamond; proceeds from the July 1908 game went toward the building of a library.

wood Union High School District was formed in 1903, uniting the Cahuenga, Laurel, Coldwater, Sherman, Los Feliz, Lankershim, and Pass grammar school districts. In September, the Hollywood Union High School opened in temporary quarters in one of the storage rooms on the ground floor of the new Masonic Temple located on the west side of Highland north of Hollywood Boulevard.

Thirty pupils were enrolled in the school, which had James O. Churchill as its first principal. By spring there were fifty and before the close of the first year, seventy-five were in attendance.

The cornerstone of the high school, which later dropped the word Union, was laid at the corner of Sunset and Highland on November 23, 1904. Students tethered their horses on what is now the athletic field, and a lemon grove on the west side of the school provided quite a different aroma from that created by today's Sunset Boulevard traffic. Hollywood High School has since graduated such notables as Nobel chemistry prizewinner William Shockley, Episcopal Bishop James J. Pike, actress Carol Burnett, and Norman Chandler, publisher of the *Los Angeles Times.*

Grant School and Fremont School, now Selma Avenue School, began construction while Hollywood High School was being built and as Hollywood's population grew, these grammar schools expanded. Three months after Los Angeles took Hollywood under its wing, the Gardner Street School was established at the southeast corner of Gardner and Hawthorne avenues.

Private schools also helped lift the burden from public education. In April 1905, the Sisters of the Immaculate Heart of Mary broke ground in a mustard field at Western and Franklin avenues for a motherhouse, novitiate, and girl's high school. The three-story building, which included classrooms and a dormitory, was of Mission-Moorish design with a red roof, arched porticos, and gleaming gold crosses. The school became an immediate success, drawing students from all over Southern California as well as some foreign countries. In 1908, Immaculate Heart High School became the first private school in Southern California to re-

ceive college accreditation, and since its founding the school had graduated more than 5,400 students.

Another fine private school was the Hollywood School for Girls, located at 1749 North La Brea Avenue. Founded in 1909, the school achieved a high academic standing in its college preparatory work, registering as many as 225 pupils. Among its many illustrious students were Misses Agnes DeMille, Katherine DeMille, Jean Harlow, Dorothy Sills, Catherine Toberman, and Mrs. David Selznick.

With the population of Hollywood increasing rapidly, there was growing need for more houses of worship. The First Presbyterian Chruch of Hollywood was organized in 1903, with twenty-three members. Shortly thereafter, the present site at the northeast corner of Gower and Carlos was purchased for $300 and the cornerstone laid on November 6, 1909, for a complete church structure.

Twelve years later, a committee was organized to formulate plans for a larger edifice. The first shovel of earth was turned on Easter Sunday, April 1, 1923. The membership then numbered 875. Construction became too disruptive, so the congregation simply moved to the Apollo Theater on Hollywood Boulevard. When the building, which seated 1,800, was completed on November 16, 1924, the church had spent $475,000 for the new structure and its furnishings.

The same year the Presbyterians organized, the Baptists formed the First Baptist Church with twenty-eight members. They too used the Masonic Temple for worship until 1908, when they built a small Sunday School chapel on Las Palmas Avenue. Ten years later they erected a new church, which faced Selma Avenue at Las Palmas. Destroyed by fire in 1935, it was replaced the following year with the present church edifice.

In August 1909, a few Methodists formed the First Methodist Episcopal Church of Hollywood and held meetings in Wilcox Hall. The following

In 1909, Hollywood boasted of its frostless belt, many paved streets, and no saloons; this was two years before its first movie company, the Nestor Film Company, had settled in Hollywood.

year, a beautiful stucco church was dedicated at the northeast corner of Hollywood Boulevard and Ivar Avenue, and, in 1925, a new church site was purchased at the northwest corner of Franklin and Highland avenues. Here, in 1926, was erected a recreation building, and in 1929, the cornerstone of the present church was laid. Nine years later, the name of the popular church was changed to First Methodist Church of Hollywood and, in 1968, the congregation adopted the name First United Methodist Church.

The same year the Methodists formed, a Christian Science Society was organized in Hollywood and began holding meetings in the Masonic Temple on Highland Avenue. Soon this society became the First Church of Christ, Scientists, of Hollywood, and later the Fifth Church of Christ, Scientists of Los Angeles. By 1916, the growing congregation warranted the erection of a classic edifice, with seating to accommodate 1,000, at the northwest corner of Hollywood Boulevard and La Brea Avenue.

The building served the congregation well for more than forty years. However, by the 1950s, the structure was showing its age and became too small for the church's growing membership. After a successful fund-raising campaign, demolition of the old church and building of the new edifice were started in January 1959.

Tilting Tournaments and Libraries

Hollywood's first annual Tilting Tournament and Floral Parade was held in 1907, sponsored by the two-year-old Hollywood Club, which had already become the center of the city's social activity. The tournament began at noon on April 20, when a parade of flower-decked horse and motor vehicles, flanked by horses carrying brightly costumed riders, made its way down Hollywood Boulevard. The boulevard was lined with people along the entire parade route from Highland to Cahuenga avenues. At Cahuenga, a large grand-

stand faced a judging stand situated across the street. Between the stands was a row of three posts, each with a cross arm from which hung a large, white harness ring.

Fighting just to keep their fourteen-foot lances level, riders grouped their horses across from the Hollywood Club, and, as the judges gave the word, dashed over the course, attempting to spear the rings with their unwieldy lances. The rider capturing the most rings in three rides was the winner, who chose his partner to lead the grand march at a ball later that evening.

The Women's Club of Hollywood was also organized in 1905, but set its cultural sights a bit higher. Its constitutional purpose was to be "the upbuilding of the social, intellectual, and civic life and the establishing of a public library in the city of Hollywood." The library committee immediately began working to raise funds and solicit donations of books. A book reception at the Hollywood Hotel netted 203 books and fifteen-dollars. A baseball game the following month between Hollywood merchants and real estate men netted $59.50. Over the next few months other events increased the books and the capital fund of the library. Temporary facilities were rented and furnished on Ca-

Top: Hollywood High School, 1910; the cornerstone of the high school was laid on November 23, 1904, and its newest buildings [center and right] were opened five years later. Bottom: The Los Angeles-Pacific Railroad ticket office on Hollywood Boulevard at Ivar; photo taken 1909.

huenga Avenue, just south of Hollywood Boulevard, and the Hollywood Public Library opened its
doors on February 8, 1906.

The women's club then procured a $10,000
donation from Andrew Carnegie for the construction of a library building, raised an additional
$5,000 by public subscription, and began construc-
tion of a single-story English bungalow-style library on land donated by Mrs. Beveridge on the
northwest corner of Hollywood Boulevard and
Ivar. The library opened April 1, 1907, and within
four years boasted of 3,798 cardholders. Fifteen
years later, the library was faced with the problem
of not having enough room to accommodate the
increasing number of books and cardholders. The
old library building was moved to West Hollywood and a modern Spanish-style facility was
erected in its place. This building served the Hollywood community well until the library moved, in
1940, to its present location at 1623 Ivar Avenue.

The women's club, which contributed so
much to Hollywood's library, didn't have its own
building until 1915. The women built a clubhouse
on the southeast corner of Hollywood Boulevard
and La Brea Avenue, which served until 1949
when the present clubhouse was christened at
1749 North La Brea.

Colegrove, the area directly south of Hollywood, was annexed to Los Angeles in 1909, so that
the village could share in the benefits of the outfall
sewer and the water supply from the Owens River
Aqueduct then under construction. Hollywood
thus became bounded on the south by Los Angeles.
Ever since incorporation in 1903, Hollywood had
struggled for an adequate water supply, but annexation talk at that time was vigorously opposed by
the Los Angeles Water Board because of the extra
water burden. Hollywood had successfully drilled
for water at Las Palmas and Franklin avenues, at
Selma and Hudson, on Kings Road south of Santa
Monica Boulevard, and at Sunset and Western. But
the water supply was insufficient for continued
growth.

In 1907, William Mulholland and his Los
Angeles city water system engineers outlined a

proposal to bring water 250 miles from the Owens
River Valley in the north. Los Angeles' citizens
voted the necessary bonds in two elections, even
though the cost would be $24,500,000. Work was
started in 1908. Water seemed assured and Los
Angeles' attitude toward annexation changed.
Nearby densely populated county territories
hastened to merge with the growing metropolis.

Hollywood's population also had grown too
dense to depend on cesspools. Surrounding areas
were too valuable for sewer farms or septic tanks,
and the distance to the sea was too great to consider the cost of an outfall sewer. Annexation to
Los Angeles would assure water and adequate
drainage through the city's outfall sewer. The election was held in 1910. It was an overwhelming victory for annexation.

Hollywood's street numbers now had to be
changed. Prior to annexation, all street numbers in
Hollywood began with 100 running the four
compass points from the intersection of Hollywood and Cahuenga boulevards. After annexation,

Top [1910]: Horse-drawn wagons are loaded and ready to deliver; the iceman's arrival was a summertime highlight for youngsters, who were given shavings from the big blocks of ice; customers signified the amount of ice desired by placing "ice cards" in their windows. Bottom: President William Howard Taft stands at an open street car window during his visit to Hollywood in 1910.

Top: Unidentified city engineers and surveyors gather before the Hollywood City Hall in 1910; this same building, located on the west side of Cahuenga south of Hollywood Boulevard, was originally occupied by the police department. Bottom: In 1910, the Sunset Livery & Boarding Stable was the site of the first electric sign in Hollywood; cowboy stars and stuntmen who stayed at the Sackett Hotel [a block north] kept their horses here and rode them to work each morning at the movie studios.

the 100 block of Cahuenga became the 1700 block and the 100 block of Hollywood Boulevard became the 6400 block.

One of the last official acts of Hollywood's Board of Trustees was to change the name of Prospect Avenue to Hollywood Boulevard. At about the same time, many of the streets were renamed to honor the early settlers.

Origin Of Some Hollywood Street Names

Ambrose Street:
  Ambrose Gregory, rancher
Barton Avenue:
  Barton Jones, grandson of Senator Cole
Beachwood Drive:
  Albert Beach, subdivider of Beachwood Canyon
Cahuenga Avenue:
  Cahuenga Pass
Carlton Way:
  Carlton Warner, son of subdivider
Carmen Avenue:
  Carmen Lopez, son of Presidencia Lopez, rancher
Colegrove:
  Maiden name of Senator Cole's wife
Cole Street:
  Senator Cornelius Cole, founder of Colegrove

Curson Avenue:
  Elijah Curson, subdivider
DeLongpre Avenue:
  Paul DeLongpre, artist
El Centro:
  Center of the Cole ranch
Eleanor Street:
  Eleanor Cole, daughter of Seward Cole
Finley Avenue:
  Reverend Finley, Methodist minister
Gardner Street:
  Dr. Alan Gardner
Gower Street:
  G.T. Gower, west line of ranch
Gregory Street:
  Ambrose Gregory, rancher
Harold Way:
  Harold Warner, son of subdivider
Hayvenhurst Avenue:
  Mr. Andrew Hay, subdivider
Highland Avenue:
  Maiden name of Mrs. Walter Price
Hudson Avenue:
  Thomas Hudson, rancher
Ivar Avenue:
  Ivar Weid, Danish owner of Weid ranch
Lodi Place:
  Lodi, New York, birthplace of Senator Cole
McCadden Place:
  W.C. McCadden, subdivider
Miller Avenue:
  Jacob Miller, rancher
Nichols Canyon:
  Mayor John G. Nichols
Ogden Avenue:
  Mrs. Mary B. Ogden, pioneer
Santa Monica Boulevard:
  Road to Santa Monica

The home of artist Paul De Longpre, on the northwest corner of Hollywood and Cahuenga, was the city's first tourist attraction.

Tunnel Day

On September 23, 1909, just a few weeks before Hollywood was annexed to the city of Los Angeles, Hollywood celebrated Tunnel Day. Until then, the Pacific Electric car line between Hollywood and Los Angeles followed Sunset Boulevard to the Plaza, south on Spring Street to the retail business center at Seventh Street. Due largely to the efforts of the board of trade, the railroad company was at last induced to construct the Hill Street Tunnel, which reduced the time to Hollywood by twelve minutes. The ribbon was cut and the first car arrived in Hollywood at 1:00 P.M., where it found the boulevard in bunting, the home and studio of Paul DeLongpre profusely decorated with flags and flowers, and committees of the women's club and the board of trade in the receiving line. The showplaces of the city kept open house, and cars manned by citizens carried the guests to points of interest—the outpost of General Otis; Laughlin Park with its wealth of exotic plants,

59

Top: Cecil B. DeMille [at right, with English riding boots] and the entire cast of *Squaw Man*, in front of the ''DeMille Barn''; 1913.

Photo by J.A.Ramsey
Dingman Studio

Bottom: Cars of the Universal Film Manufacturing Company Garage, at 6652 Sunset, 1913.

bananas, and graceful palms; Sturtevant's water lilies; Rapp's pineapple orchard; Glen Holly's rose gardens; Whitley Heights with its panorama of city and sea; and the winding lanes of Laurel Canyon. Cars from Los Angeles arrived every five minutes from 1:00 P.M. to 5:00 P.M. Twelve minutes cut from the time to Los Angeles proved to be a great boon to Hollywood.

Law and Order

Shortly after Hollywood was incorporated as a city of the sixth class, Daeida Wilcox Beveridge donated a lot on Cahuenga Avenue, just south of Hollywood Boulevard, for use as the city hall and police department. A small, two-room wood-frame bungalow was erected, which housed the police department, city engineer and city clerk.

The police force, which consisted of two officers, originally made their calls on horseback, but as time wore on, they "raced to the scene" on bicycles.

Three years after Hollywood was annexed to the city of Los Angeles, the Sixth Division of the Los Angeles Police Department was established and assigned to the two-room station with Sergeant E. Carpenter in charge. In 1913, a modern structure was built at 1625-29 North Cahuenga Avenue, next to the old police department bungalow, and served as both the fire and police department. The following year, the force of twenty peace officers answered 1,948 calls and made 247 arrests.

With the increase in both pedestrian and vehicular traffic, the division grew rapidly and was augmented by several traffic officers. Their job was to control intersections in the absence of mechanically controlled signals. It wasn't until the mid-Twenties that these signals were installed on the busier corners.

Traffic officers were identified by a patch worn on their shoulder, showing a horse head superimposed over a wagon wheel. On Sunday afternoons, three officers worked a standard assignment. One was transported to the top of Cahuenga Pass, another was stationed halfway down the hill,

and a third was placed at the bottom. Since the pass consisted of a single-lane road with a small stream at the side, their duty was to assist stalled motorists and direct others who were touring between the San Fernando Valley and Hollywood. Their primary purpose was to keep the lane open so others could continue their journey.

Patrol officers utilized several vehicles referred to as jitneys and it was required that all jitney officers should ring in on a Gamewell box every fifteen minutes to receive their calls and relay information. Radio cars were still a dream of the future and were not to come into being until the mid-1930s.

The foot-beat officers reported every half hour by giving their box number and pulling a handle activating a tape in the station, which would record the ring. Supplementing the jitneys were the detective vehicles, or "fast cars." These were even equipped with red lights and sirens, while the jitney cars had none. When something calling for quick action occurred, the detectives would jump in their fast cars and race to the scene. Jitney officers obviously had to use their ingenuity after honking their horns failed to persuade citizens to pull to the side.

Prior to annexation, all firefighting had been performed by volunteer firemen, who drove and operated horse-drawn fire equipment. Shortly after

Top: Looking north at the Hollywood Hotel in 1910; the street at right is Highland; the hotel was built in 1903 and was razed in 1956. Bottom: The building of the Pacific Electric railroad line through the Cahuenga Pass in 1911.

Hollywood was annexed to the city of Los Angeles in 1910, the city established a firehouse, known as Hose Company No. 7, at the southeast corner of Cahuenga and Selma avenues. Under the command of Chief Jack Atwell, the small station housed the first motorized piece of firefighting apparatus in the city of Los Angeles.

As mentioned earlier, the city built a combination police and fire station in 1914, located at 1625-29 Cahuenga Avenue. When Hose Company No. 7 moved to the new location, its designation was changed to Engine Company No. 27. At the same time, additional firefighting apparatus was acquired. Firefighters called this home until 1930, when they and the police department moved to new and separate locations.

Four Hillside Mansions

By now Hollywood had become famous from coast to coast for its beautiful hillside homes, and it soon was to boast of four more architectural treasures. The first of these was Glengarry Castle, built in 1909 at the northeast corner of Franklin and Argyle by a retired Chicago doctor, A.G. Schloesser. The mansion was reminiscent of Glengarry Castle in Scotland and Nuremburg Castle in Germany. The enormous rooms and halls were filled with authentic armor, tapestries, marble statues, antique furniture, and other priceless art objects.

Dr. Schloesser [who later changed the family name to Castles because of the anti-German sentiments during World War II] built another hillside mansion three years later just across Argyle from Glengarry Castle. He called it Sans Souci Castle and it suggested the German Rhine castles and the gothic halls of baronial England. As with Glengarry, Sans Souci Castle was filled with artworks and for years was a great tourist attraction.

The third hillside mansion was built by Rollin B. Lane on Franklin Avenue at the head of Orange Drive and christened Holly Chateau by Mrs. Lane. This three-story, seventeen-room home was designed in Victorian style on the outside and a variety of styles inside. The Lanes lived in the house

until they died. Eventually it was sold to Tom Glover Sr., who leased it in 1961 to Milt and Bill Larson, who restored and remodeled it and resurrected the mansion as the Magic Castle, a private club whose members now include a thousand magicians.

Adolph and Eugene Bernheimer, leading New York importers of Oriental goods, arrived in Hollywood in 1908 and bought seven acres on the crest of a high hill behind the Lane mansion, where they built a home reminiscent of the mansions of lordly Japanese rulers. The Bernheimer's Palace on the Hill—Yamashiro—was completed in 1914. Adolph Bernheimer sold the home in 1923, after his brother died. Over the next twenty years the property passed through several hands, declining to a state of disrepair until Tom Glover Sr. acquired it in 1949. Glover embarked on an extensive restoration program, which, when completed, allowed the public to enjoy the original beauty of the palace and beautifully manicured gardens. During the past twenty years, the Yamashiro has been the backdrop for such films and television productions as *Sayonara*, "Hollywood Backstage," and "I Spy." Today it is operated solely as a restaurant, offering with its cuisine a breathtaking panoramic view of Hollywood.

Another famous residence was purchased by Herman Janes, who came to Hollywood in 1903 with his wife, Mary, and their four children, Grace, Mabel, Carrie, and Donald. They bought one of H.J. Whitley's newly constructed homes at 6541 Hollywood Boulevard, where, in 1911, Mrs. Janes assisted her three daughters in starting the Misses Janes School. Over the next fifteen years more than a thousand children got at least part of their elementary education there. The roll call of the Misses Janes School included the children of many stage and screen celebrities such as Cecil B. Demille, Jesse Lasky, Thomas Ince, Noah Beery, Jack Holt, and Richard Arlen. The Janes' home stands today, the oldest surviving structure in Hollywood and the only remaining residence on Hollywood Boulevard between Vermont and La Brea avenues.

George Eastman [arm resting on front seat], an early Hollywood pioneer and businessman, with his employees; photo taken 1911.

Mr. Hollywood

One of Hollywood's most prominent pioneers and citizens is Charles Edward Toberman. Born in Seymour, Texas, on February 23, 1880, he was educated at Texas A & M College and Metropolitan Business College. Five years after his marriage to Josephine Bullock on March 15, 1902, they moved to Hollywood, where his uncle, the former mayor of Los Angeles, James R. Toberman, resided. Shortly thereafter, Mr. Toberman went into the real estate and insurance business with B.C. Edwards. Two months later, the partnership was dissolved and Mr. Toberman formed the C.E. Toberman Company, which immediately acquired a 10 x 10-foot building for $100 at the southeast corner of Prospect and Highland avenues. Later, he built a 15 x 20-foot brick building on the southwest corner of Prospect Avenue and Dakota Street [now McCadden Place], where he relocated his business. This marked the beginning of a long and successful career for the man who, years later, became known as "Mr. Hollywood."

During the next seventy years, Mr. Toberman placed fifty-three Hollywood subdivisions on the market, formed more than thirty companies and organizations, built twenty-nine commercial buildings in Hollywood, including the world-famous Chinese Theater, and was affiliated with forty-nine clubs, civic, and fraternal organizations. Today, at ninety-nine years of age, Mr. Toberman still actively manages his real estate holdings from his office in the heart of Hollywood.

Lookout Mountain

Laurel Canyon became a popular scenic location shortly after Hollywood was annexed to Los Angeles. Hundreds of visitors each week traveled up the two-mile-long Laurel Canyon Boulevard, a graded dirt road. The road ran up the canyon, where it divided at what is now Lookout Mountain Avenue. The left road twisted to the summit of Lookout Mountain, while the right road continued

Above [1913]: Los Feliz School
on Hollywood Boulevard,
just west of Vermont. At right:
Students of Grant School, 1912.

to the top of the Santa Monica Mountains and down to the San Fernando Valley.

In 1908, Lookout Mountain was subdivided into bungalow lots, most of which had panoramic views of the city. The winding dirt road to the top of the mountain was widened in 1910 and the Lookout Mountain Inn was built. The inn consisted of twenty-four rooms, a bandstand, and a pavilion. Diners enjoying the inn's chicken dinner specialty had an unobstructed 270-degree view of Los Angeles—worth the forty-five-minute drive up the steep grade in their underpowered automobiles.

A subdivision known as Bungalow Land was built at the Lookout Mountain turnoff at about the same time as the inn. To stimulate its development, a trackless trolley service was begun from Sunset and Laurel Avenue to a tavern at the Lookout Mountain junction. The trackless trolley ran up and down Laurel Canyon every half hour between 7:45 A.M. and 11:15 P.M. for six years. The trolley sometimes labored up the steep grade at no more than four miles an hour, and, when two cars met, the operator of the car heading down the hill had to stop and remove his contactors from the single pair of overhead wires to let the upward-

Top: Cows graze on the site of a 1924 subdivision on Hollywood Boulevard west of La Brea. Bottom: C.E. Toberman in his real estate office on the southwest corner of Hollywood Boulevard and McCadden Place; a pioneer and entrepreneur, Toberman was such a tireless fund raiser and master builder that he was nicknamed "Mr. Hollywood" by his Hollywood contemporaries.

bound trolley pass. The Lookout Mountain Inn was destroyed by fire in 1918, and the trolley service was discontinued at about the same time because of insufficient patronage.

Late in 1911, A.P. Warrington arrived in Hollywood in search of a home for the American branch of the Theosophical Society, of which branch he was president. After weeks of searching,

The Masons moved into this temple, on the west side of Highland, a block north of Hollywood Boulevard, in 1904.

he finally purchased the south slope of the hill between Argyle and Gower, north of the north end of Carmen and Vista del Mar avenues. Here he soon erected several Spanish-and-Moorish-style buildings among the orange and lemon trees and tropical foliage, creating a center that was long known as Krotona. Public lectures were given Sunday afternoons, while adult courses were given in theosophy, philosophy, astrology, and psychology to fill the gap between scientific and theosophical education. For a number of years, their community thrived and became a considerable factor in the commercial life of Hollywood, though the members kept much to themselves socially.

The Movies
Come To Hollywood

Bad weather in Chicago during 1907 forced Colonel William Selig, head of the Selig Polyscope Company, to send a film company to the southwest to film scenes for *The Count of Monte Cristo.* Director Francis Boggs, a cameraman, and six actors and actresses filmed in Los Angeles and on the beach at Santa Monica, then moved on to Colorado. But the weather there proved no more stable than Chicago's, and, in 1909, the Selig company returned to Los Angeles.

Boggs rented a vacant Chinese laundry at the corner of Eighth and Olive streets, converted the building into dressing rooms and an office, and built a 40-foot-square stage on the lot next door.

There he filmed *The Heart of a Race Tout,* the first movie to be made completely in California. It was released on July 27, 1909.

Selig realized that the predictable weather and variety of landscapes immediately available made the Los Angeles area ideal for the making of moving pictures. He moved from Chicago and built a permanent studio in Edendale. Four years later, he built the Selig Zoo, which then became his studio and the location of most of his films. Glendale Boulevard, then called Allesandro Avenue, ran through the center of Edendale, which quickly became the site of half a dozen movie companies located on either side of the avenue.

Shortly after Selig's troup arrived in Los Angeles, other motion picture companies began to migrate West. The New York Motion Picture Company settled in Edendale in 1909, and later set up shop in the Santa Monica Mountains. Biograph established a studio in Los Angeles; Essanay Company moved to Niles, California; and the Kalem Company settled near Glendale.

The distinction of having established the first studio in Hollywood goes to the Nestor Film Company of Bayonne, New Jersey. Forty members of this company headed by David Horsley, arrived by train on October 27, 1911. On the train, Horsley met Murray Steele, who advised him to call upon Frank Hoover, a Hollywood photographer, for information on light conditions in Hollywood. Horsely did just that and the next day he was shown the former Blondeau Tavern on the northwest corner of Sunset and Gower. The small roadhouse, suffering from Hollywood's recent liquor prohibition ordinance, had a barn, corral, twelve small single-room structures built along a fence, and a five-room bungalow.

Horsely leased the tavern for thirty-dollars a month and used the corral for horses used in westerns, the barn for props, the small rooms for dressing areas, and the bungalow for his executive offices. A baggage car carrying three cameras, chemicals, and some props arrived in Hollywood the following Monday, was unloaded overnight, and the company was ready to shoot. Horsley's

Above and left: The trackless
trolley that ran on Laurel
Canyon Road from Sunset to
Lookout Mountain Road.
The trolley began operation
in 1912 as part of a real
estate development plan; it
ran for several years and
was mechanically sound, but
it was discontinued because
of insufficient patronage.
The top photo was taken in
1915; the bottom in 1914.

budget, allocated by New York, was $1,200 a week, and three complete pictures were supposed to be filmed each week: a western, an eastern, and a comedy. Stories were written at home each evening and scenes were allocated a specified film footage. Action was rehearsed carefully by stopwatch, and when the scene had been timed to the number of feet of film available, the camera was loaded and filming began.

There was neither time nor money to have prints made, so Horsley's directors would cut the negatives and ship them to New York for printing and release, often not seeing their own work until two or three months later when the picture finally came to the Idyl Hour Theater, Hollywood's first. The Idyl Hour was established in either late 1910 or early 1911 at 6525 Hollywood Boulevard. During its first year the theater was little more than a converted store with chairs, a projector, and a screen. The Idyl Hour, whose name was changed to the Iris Theater in 1913, moved to 6415 Hollywood Boulevard in 1914, and to a new 1,000-seat theater at 6508 Hollywood Boulevard in 1918.

Cecil B. DeMille [on running board] with some of the actors from his movie *The Squaw Man*; this photo was taken in 1914.

The second theater was, appropriately, the Hollywood Theater. It opened in 1913, had a capacity of 700 and charged ten cents for general admission, fifteen cents for loge seats and a nickel for children. At those prices it prospered and today it is the oldest theater in Hollywood.

The Nestor Company's first stage consisted of a wooden platform about forty feet square. Because most scenes were filmed outdoors, large sheets of muslin were suspended about fifteen feet above the stage, in order to diffuse the intense sunlight.

On occasions when two production companies tried to shoot on the same stage, one background was built on the north side and one on the east side of the stage. Everything worked fine unless one of the two directors happened to forget himself and walk across the camera lines to his actors and thus burst into the other director's picture.

The first picture made at Hollywood's first

studio was *The Law of the Range,* written by Alexandra Fahrney and directed by her husband, Milton. Other early films produced by Nestor included *Her Indian Hero,* and the *Mutt and Jeff* and *Desperate Desmond* series.

The Nestor Film Company discovered it could churn out picture after picture in Hollywood with few delays from bad weather. Other companies, enduring the erratic climate of the East, marveled at Nestor's steady output and improved photographic quality, and came to Hollywood to learn the secret. Within months, fifteen companies were shooting in and around Hollywood.

There was another reason besides weather for the mass migration. In the East, movie companies were wallowing in a morass of suits, injunctions, raids, and riots that had begun in 1897, when Thomas Edison started suing independent producers for patent infringment. As the "flickers" supplanted shooting galleries and penny arcades in popularity, producers licensed by Edison formed the Motion Picture Patents Company, widely known as The Trust, to safeguard their claims to film profits. The Trust included Edison's Vitagraph, Lubin, Selig, Essanay, Kalem, Pathe, and Melies. Its monopoly, however, was threatened by a group of small producers and exhibitors who, having been excluded from The Trust, began to construct or import bootleg equipment to make their pictures in obscure hideouts. The Trust waged one of the most vigorous battles in the history of American industrialism against these independents. The pirates fled from New York to Florida to Cuba and, finally, to California, followed shortly by the trust companies, who were attracted by the same climate and topography. In California, the pirates stood their ground and fought back and, ultimately, The Trust languished.

In May 1912, Carl Laemmle formed the Universal Film Manufacturing Company, which then acquired the Nestor Film Company, as well as the property to the south, across the street. The next year, Universal leased 250 acres of the former Taylor Ranch in the San Fernando Valley and, in March 1915, Laemmle abandoned the studio at

Top: The Kalem Company, 1425 Hoover Street [now KCET-TV].
Bottom: The entire film company posed for this 1915 photo.

Sunset and Gower and officially opened his Universal City.

The former Nestor studio was taken over by Fred Balshofer for his Quality Pictures Company. His tenancy only lasted one year, as the facility changed hands in 1916 to Charles and Al Christie's "Christie Comedies," who continued to occupy the studio until 1930.

Cecil B. DeMille, Jesse Lasky, Samuel Goldfish, and Arthur Friend formed the Jesse L. Lasky Feature Play Company in New York in 1913, and persuaded Dustin Farnum, one of the biggest stars of the day, to appear in their first film, *The Squaw Man.* DeMille, Farnum, and a small troup headed West in December to begin filming. They planned to make the film in Flagstaff, Arizona, but when they arrived, they found the scenery unsuitable for their needs, so they reboarded the train and continued on to Hollywood, where DeMille rented a portion of a small barn at the southeast corner of Vine and Selma, across the street from the site now

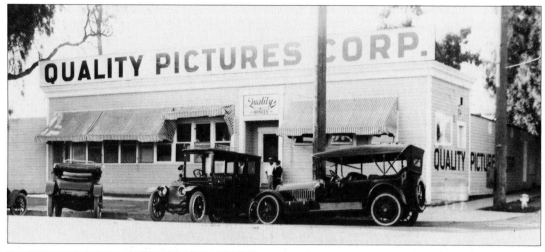

occupied by American Savings, which is commonly thought to have been the site of the barn. The bank even bears a plaque commemorating the misconception.

DeMille moved into one side of the barn, while the owner, Jacob Stern, kept his horses in the other half. Whenever the horses were watered, the water ran into DeMille's office and he was forced to wear galoshes or put his feet in the wastebasket. *The Squaw Man* was made on a budget of $15,000 and earned more than $225,000. Within eighteen months, the Lasky studio occupied the entire block and by the end of the decade it occupied two full blocks.

The Jesse L. Lasky Feature Play Company merged with Adolph Zukor's Famous Players Film Company in 1916 to form Famous Players-Lasky

Quality Pictures occupied the former Nestor Studio at Sunset and Gower [northwest corner] in 1915; the following year, the studio was occupied by the Christie Film Company, whose actors and personnel are shown above. Actor Francis X. Bushman began his noteworthy film career with Quality Pictures Corporation.

Corporation. Zukor had assembled many fine actors, including a young Canadian girl named Gladys Smith, who took the screen name Mary Pickford and became "America's Sweetheart." Samuel Goldfish left Famous Players-Lasky to form a partnership with Edgar Selwyn. Combining syllables from each of their surnames, they called the new company Goldwyn Pictures Corporation. Goldfish later changed his own name to Goldwyn and was instrumental in the founding of Metro-Goldwyn-Mayer and the Samuel Goldwyn Studios.

After a short stay at the Biograph Film Company, a young director named D.W. Griffith began

making movies at the Majestic Reliance Studios at 4500 Sunset Boulevard. The Triangle Film Corporation was formed by Griffith, Thomas Ince, and Mack Sennett in 1915 and Griffith took over the Majestic Reliance Studio, renaming it the Fine Arts Studio. Here Griffith made his spectacular film, *Intolerance,* in 1916. He erected the film's enormous Babylon set on vacant property across the street. The set loomed over the residences surrounding the studio for years.

Another pioneer film producer was the Vitagraph Company, founded by J. Stuart Blackton and Albert E. Smith. Seeking more "western-type" settings and an environment which would allow year-round "shooting," a troupe from Vitagraph left the East for California on October 23, 1911. The party arrived in Los Angeles a month later and the following day established a studio in Santa Monica. They immediately launched a program of making one-reel westerns, producing an average of

Top: Workmen put the finishing touches on the colossal sets of D.W. Griffith's classic film *Intolerance;* the sets remained standing for three years after the film was completed. Bottom: Mack Sennett built this studio for Mabel Normand at Fountain Avenue and Bates Street; her company produced one film before Mabel Normand signed with Goldwyn, and Mack Sennett leased the vacant studio in 1917 to western film star William S. Hart.

SUPPLEMENT

HOLLYWOOD CITIZEN

Vol. VII.   HOLLYWOOD, CALIFORNIA, FRIDAY, MARCH 8, 1912.   No. 48

HOLLYWOOD

The Beautiful Foothill Suburb Overlooking Los Angeles and the Sea

LILY POND OF E. D. STURTEVANT

ANNUAL PROGRESS EDITION

Hollywood Police Station, 1916; the station was on the west side of Cahuenga Avenue, just south of Hollywood Boulevard. Right: The Van Griffith Auto Service. Van was the son of Griffith J. Griffith, for whom Griffith Park was named; 1914.

about one picture per week.

After five years of residing and filming in Santa Monica, the Vitagraph Company purchased approximately twenty-five acres at Prospect and Talmadge avenues in Hollywood. Here they erected a large studio and turned out countless films starring such celebrities as Norma Talmadge, Anita Stewart, and Larry Semon. During the years of peak production, there were as many as five hundred people on the lot each day, earning salaries from $100 to $5,000 a week. In addition to grinding out numerous westerns, they specialized in producing three-reel serial features.

The Vitagraph Company passed out of existence in February of 1925, when Albert E. Smith sold the entire company to Harry Warner of Warner Brothers. The lot was renamed Warner Brothers-Vitagraph Studio and it was here that many of the Warner Brothers spectacular movies were filmed.

One of the lesser known, but oldest, studios in Hollywood is located at the corner of Sunset and Hoover. The studio is still standing and has been occupied by eleven small movie companies since it was established in 1912 by a group affiliated with the Lubin Manufacturing Company. Lubin's days in Hollywood were few, however, and the studio was taken over by the Essanay Company, co-founded and owned by George K. Spoor and Bronco Billy Anderson [S and A]. Essanay made twenty-one westerns at the studio in almost as many weeks, then abandoned it to return to its home in Niles. The Kalem Company occupied the studio for four years from 1913 to 1917. Companies that followed Kalem were Willis and Ingles, J.D. Hampton, Charles Ray, Ralph Like, Monogram, Allied Artists, and Colorvision. Today it is the home of KCET, Los Angeles' public television station, which bought it in 1970.

Just prior to the Twenties, the film-going public began to demand not only feature productions but stars. Up in marquee lights went such names as John Bunny, Flora Finch, Lottie Brisco, Grace Cunard, Helen Holmes, Arthur Johnson, Marguerite Clark, Blanche Sweet, Tom Mix, Anita

The Fine Arts Studio, also known as Griffith Studios, was at the junction of Hollywood and Sunset boulevards; photo 1917.

Stewart, Earle Williams, William S. Hart, Charles Ray, Norma and Constance Talmadge, Wallace Reid, Ben Lyon, and Bebe Daniels, as well as the Gish sisters—Dorothy, who wore a pink ribbon, and Lillian, who wore blue, so their director, Griffith, could tell them apart.

Hollywood, the quiet suburb of stately residences built among the lemon groves of the foothill frostless belt, underwent a wondrous change. Great barnlike studio structures popped up overnight among the beautiful homes, causing consternation among the residents and resulting in the passage of zoning ordinances, which continue to be argued over by citizens and studios even today. With a population of 500 at the turn of the twentieth century, Hollywood had grown to 700 in 1903, to 4,000 in 1909, and to 7,500 in 1913, primarily because of the movie business. Hollywood Boulevard was lined with stores that sold the latest styles and fashions in merchandise.

Scenes then, as now, were shot all over Hollywood. Private homes were used for domestic dramas. Banks were used on holidays, Saturday afternoons, and Sundays for hold-up scenes. Stores were robbed regularly before the cameras. Citizens were stopped on the streets to augment mob scenes. Streets were roped off for automobile accidents. Christie's Bathing Beauties would rush down the street in costume to their favorite restaurant for a between-acts' lunch.

This perpetual public vaudeville brought the tourists to fill more hotels and restaurants. Many tried to find the eating places of their favorite star,

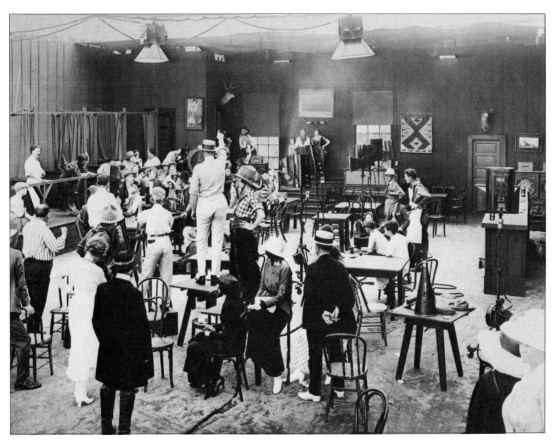

Above: The studio and actors are unidentified, but the genre is unmistakable; hundreds of westerns were cranked out in Hollywood's early days; this photo was taken in 1918. At right: One of the early front offices of Metro Studios at Lillian Way and Eleanor Street; when Metro vacated for larger quarters, Buster Keaton rented it to produce his own films; photo taken 1918.

mistook each other for the personality sought, and left with curiosity satisfied.

The city grew. Lemon acreage bought for $700 became $10,000 per acre subdivision property. The name of Hollywood became known throughout the world. Neighboring areas envied Hollywood's publicity and adopted the name. Toluca and Lankershim became North Hollywood, Prospect Park became East Hollywood, Colegrove became South Hollywood, while West Hollywood took in Sherman as far west as Beverly Hills.

More Churches

During the Teens, several more churches were added to the already fine list of religious houses. Two of these additions were St. Thomas Episcopal Church and the Hollywood Congregational Church. The first of these two, St. Thomas, was established as a mission in April 1914. After meeting for years in a theater, grocery store, and a real estate office, a lot was purchased at the southwest corner of Sunset Boulevard and Sierra Bonita and a frame church erected. In 1921, the frame building was moved to the present church location at the northwest corner of Hollywood Boulevard and Gardner Street. Within a few years, the congregation had outgrown the small building, so ground was broken for the present gothic-style church on August 17, 1930.

In 1954, the present parish hall was built, which includes church offices, Sunday School rooms, and a modern auditorium. 1971 was a glorious year for the congregation of approximately 400 baptized members, for it was then that the mortgage was burned, leaving them debt free.

Two months after St. Thomas was founded, the first service of the Hollywood Congregational Church was held at the Hollywood Theater. Five years later ground-breaking ceremonies were held for a permanent church at Hollywood Boulevard and Sycamore Avenue.

The church grew steadily, and by December of 1925, there were 700 members and about 600 in the church school. On November 16, 1947, the

thirtieth anniversary of service of their minister, Dr. James Lash, the congregation laid the cornerstone for Lash Chapel. The following years saw a number of ministers serve the congregation, which, at one point, reached 1,000 members.

As the community grew, so did the need for a place for the youth of Hollywood to gather for organized activities. To fill this need, a group of businessmen purchased a lot on the southwest corner of Selma and Hudson avenues and in 1914 founded the Hollywood YMCA. During the next few years, the necessary funds were raised to build a physical education department, dining room, kitchen, and dormitory. Fifty years later, a major expansion and renovation program was completed,

The Hollywood Theater [far left of photo] opened December 20, 1913 at 6764 Hollywood Boulevard; the city's first movie house.

which provided a comprehensive health, fitness and recreational center to serve Hollywood businessmen, as well as the youth and young adults of the community.

The Studio Club

Within a few years after the movie industry settled in Hollywood, the once-sleepy little community was inundated with hundreds of young girls from all over the country who had high hopes of instant stardom. In 1916, some of the girls began gathering regularly in the basement of the Hollywood Public Library to read plays together. The girls were strangers, lonely in an unfamiliar city, and often desperately discouraged. Eleanor Jones, the librarian, became concerned about the girls' welfare when she learned that most of them were living in poorly supervised boarding houses and cheap hotels. She and Mrs. Charles Richmond took the problem to the Young Women's Christian Association, which backed them in locating a recreation hall on Hollywood Boulevard, where the girls could meet and dance or participate in gymnastics. It was so successful that plans were made to enlarge the facilities and provide living quarters.

The funds for the first year's rent for a club-

Below: Looking west down Hollywood Boulevard toward High- | Top: The city's first public library [flag flying from window] was
land at the C.E. Toberman Building; the first two floors housed | located on the northwest corner of Hollywood and Ivar; the
offices; the top floors were apartments; photo taken in 1915. | building on the opposite corner is the First Methodist Church.

The Lookout Mountain Inn was famous for its 270-degree view; it burned down in a canyon fire in 1918; photo taken in 1915.

house at 6129 Carlos Avenue were raised in less than an hour at a businessmen's lunch. The building accommodated ten girls, among them Carmel Myers, Marjorie Daw, Zasu Pitts, and Ann O'Neal, all "extras" at the time. The building was called the Hollywood Studio Club. Ten years after its founding, the club moved into a beautiful three-story mediterranean-style structure at 1215 Lodi Place. The building had a capacity of ninety-four girls and it was filled from nearly the first day. Often there was a long waiting list. Over the next sixty years, the Hollywood Studio Club was home to thousands of girls. Most of the potential starlets had to settle for more mundane jobs, but many made the climb to stardom, including Marie Windsor, Marilyn Monroe, Dorothy Malone, Gale Storm, Linda Darnell, Barbara Eden, Kim Novak, Donna Reed, and Barbara Rush.

By the 1960s, most of the studios had left Hollywood, while changing lifestyles made the protective atmosphere of the YWCA less attractive. The club closed its doors in 1975, when the city of Los Angeles informed the YWCA that the building did not meet new fire-safety standards and could no longer be used as a residence.

Hollywood Officers Training Camp

Soon after President Wilson declared war on Germany in April 1917, C.C. Craig and Raymond Wells organized the Hollywood Officers Training Camp, which met above a garage on Hollywood Boulevard near Hudson Street. Craig and Wells planned originally to confine its membership to sixty, but that number quickly doubled. Quarters were moved to the athletic field of Hollywood High School and finally to a 20-acre tract at the corner of Melrose and Western, where offices were built and a large tent erected. Soon the camp's membership was 2,000.

The chairman of the Hollywood draft board, G.G. Greenwood, furnished the names of boys subject to the draft, who then were invited to take preliminary training at the camp. Most of them did and 137 were admitted to the Reserve Officers Training Corps and received commissions. Members of the camp furnished their rifles and instru-

Top: Horse-drawn graders work on Sunset Boulevard to prepare the land for residential subdivisions; photograph, 1918. Bottom: Rompage's Hardware Store, at 5506 Hollywood Boulevard, was a browser's delight, where one could keep abreast of all the new inventions, such as the power washer in the foreground; 1915.

ments for their band, and E.L. Doheny equipped one company with machine guns.

When Johnny came marching home to Hollywood after the war, it was to a thriving metropolis eager to continue the headlong growth that had taken place before the war. What had seemed like an explosion of growth over the past two decades turned out to be only the lighting of the fuse. The biggest boom was yet to come!

Hollywood Gets a College

In 1916, eleven years after the groundbreaking ceremonies for Immaculate Heart High School, the state granted a charter to Immaculate Heart College, empowering it to grant degrees in the arts, letters, sciences, and music. During the early years, college classes were held in the high school building at the corner of Western and Franklin avenues. But in 1927, a bungalow was built on the hill overlooking the turn of the road at Western Avenue, and it became the first college building.

Although the school was incorporated as a senior college, it didn't offer third- and fourth-year courses until 1927. The ten-year delay was caused by several factors, including the limited Catholic population and the few women who pursued four-year college educations at the time.

Building the bungalow removed the college's twenty-three acres from taxation and made possible further development. Two years later the administration building was built; the laying of its cornerstone on April 14, 1929, marked the beginning of a new era in the development of the college, and the first four-year class was graduated in June of 1929.

Top: Oriental decor and art treasures made the Bernheimer residence the most opulent in all of Hollywood; photo, 1918. Left: The Bernheimer estate as it appeared in 1925; located in the hills above the northern end of Sycamore Avenue, the former home is now the Yamashiro Restaurant, with a panoramic view of Hollywood to the south.

Above: The first Studio Club was established in 1916, at 6129 Carlos Avenue, for aspiring young actresses who were drawn from all parts of the country by the burgeoning movie business. The young ladies pictured in this 1917 photo are unidentified, but among the first boarders were then unknown extras like Zasu Pitts, Carmel Myers, Marjorie Daw, and Ann O'Neal. The Studio Club was moved to Lodi Place in 1926. At left: Modern moving vans of the Hollywood Fireproof Storage Company; photo taken in 1916.

Part Two:
1919-1938

employed thousands of people, with a total payroll of $25 million a year. The industry had been active in Hollywood for seven years by 1918. By that time, movies had established themselves as the most accessible, and therefore dominant, form of mass entertainment in America, pushing aside the vaudeville acts, concert singers, and stage plays that toured the country. Filmmakers were creating "features," running an hour or more, as well as the one- and two-reelers that had been the entertainment staple.

Poverty Row & Gower Gulch

During the late Teens and early Twenties scores of small independent studios were operating in Hollywood, primarily on Sunset Boulevard near Gower Street. These studios struggled to exist by making one- and two-reel comedies, westerns, and dramas. Because of the fierce competition, uncertainty of having their films distributed, and the difficulty of making a profit, many of these small studios went out of business as quickly as they were conceived. The high mortality rate of these independent studios caused this area of Hollywood to become known as Poverty Row.

During the same period, many extras and "movie cowboys" could be seen standing near the corner of Sunset and Gower, awaiting casting calls to appear in early western films being ground out daily by the many small production companies. To the residents of Hollywood, this area was popularly called Gower Gulch.

Some of the Poverty Row and Gower Gulch production companies that have long since passed into oblivion were Loftus Features, L-Ko Motion Picture Company, Sterling Motion Picture Company, Quality Pictures Corporation, Frances Ford Studios, Waldorf Productions, Paulis, Century

By Armistice Day, Hollywood was in the stages of a phenomenal growth cycle. Southern California's warm, sunny climate was luring the motion picture industry from the East at an accelerating rate, and was also attracting thousands of new residents. From 1910 to 1920, Hollywood's population jumped 720 percent, from 5,000 to 36,000; nine years later, the population would reach 157,000. The rest of the city of Los Angeles was growing proportionally.

In a postwar economy where fifteen to eighteen dollars a week was a good wage, prospective immigrants heard astonishing tales about Hollywood. It was said that there were people there who made $3,000 every week and who lived in hillside palaces overlooking avocado, lemon and orange groves—and oil wells.

Forty million Americans were going to the movies each week by 1920, and most of the films they saw were being produced in Hollywood by more than twenty studios. The picture business

STREET SCENE IN HOLLYWOOD

Thousands buck the line on every call issued for a few movie picture extras. This is a sample of the customary massed assault on the employment bureaus resulting from an ad for a very few men and women to work in an insignificant scene. The wage is meagre for a day or night of hard work.

Don't Try To Break Into The Movies
IN HOLLYWOOD

Until You Have Obtained Full, Frank and Dependable Information

FROM THE

HOLLYWOOD CHAMBER OF COMMERCE
(Hollywood's Great Community Organization)

It May Save Disappointments

Out of 100,000 Persons Who Started at the Bottom of the Screen's Ladder of Fame

ONLY FIVE REACHED THE TOP

Opposite page: By 1921, aspiring actors were converging on the city in such enormous numbers that the chamber of commerce was moved to take out ads in an attempt to discourage them; so seductive was the city's new industry that there was danger of being literally inundated by a sea of out-of-work humanity. Above: Famous Players-Lasky Studio, whose neat, two square block complex in the foreground is in marked contrast to the flotsam and jetsam sets of Poverty Row next to it [1920]. Left: 1921 aerial view of Hollywood mansions at the northern terminus of La Brea Avenue.

Film Company, Wilnat Studios, Wade Productions, California Studios, Bischoff Comedies, Choice Productions, Snub-Pollard Productions, Goodwill Studios, and Chadwick Pictures Company.

The Major Studios

Some studios sprang up, flourished, and merged, evolving into the giants that would eventually control the industry. In 1919, four of Hollywood's most creative film practitioners, Charles Chaplin, D.W. Griffith, Mary Pickford, and Douglas Fairbanks, created United Artists Corporation to control distribution of their own independently produced films. This action, which freed them from studio contracts, formed the first "studio" to act primarily as a distribution organization for independent production companies, a maverick position United Artists has carried to this day.

Charles Chaplin built his own studios on La Brea Avenue the year United Artists was formed.

Above: One of the first performances of the Pilgrimage Play, June 1920; Mrs. Christine Witherill Stevenson bought the canyon site, wrote the play, and journeyed to the Holy Land for authentic fabric, utensils, and props to use in its annual production. Right: An excavation at the La Brea Tar Pits, 1920.

Pickford and Fairbanks acquired a studio in 1922, when they bought the Jesse D. Hampton Studio on the south side of Santa Monica Boulevard, two blocks west of La Brea. There Fairbanks would create two of his most famous swashbuckling roles: *Robin Hood* and *The Thief of Bagdad*.

After leaving MGM, Samuel Goldwyn formed his own company in 1924 and rented space at the Pickford-Fairbanks Studio. In 1927, the year after Goldwyn became one of its partners, the studio's name was changed to United Artists. Goldwyn increased his production and studio occupancy until his company was the lot's sole occupant. As a result, the film factory's name was again changed—this time to the Samuel Goldwyn Studio, even though the majority of the ownership remained with Mary Pickford. For the next several

A group of unidentified and stylishly dressed women [and a boy]; Hollywood, 1916.

Above: A 1922 Hollywood bathing beauty contest. Right: Mary Pickford and Douglas Fairbanks pose beneath the new sign that announced their purchase of the Jesse B. Hampton Studio on Formosa Avenue [1922]; in 1927, they changed the name to United Artists; in 1948 it became the Samuel Goldwyn Studio.

years, Goldwyn and Pickford became embroiled in a highly publicized legal battle over the studio's ownership. Finally, in 1955, a court-ordered auction was held with Goldwyn being the successful bidder. At last the studio was all his.

Late in 1920, Harry and Jack Cohn and Joe Brandt decided that they had learned enough about the film business, during the years of working for the old Universal Company, to strike out on their own. They made one two-reel "short" and sold it quickly to provide money for the second. The two-reeler films became an instant success and developed into the series that became known as the Hall Room Boys Comedies. At the end of the first year, the Cohns named their firm CBC Film Sales Corporation. In 1926, after a few years of making shorts and features, CBC acquired the California Studios property at 1438 North Gower Street. At the same time, it was decided a new name was needed that was more in keeping with the dignity of a company that was making and selling successful feature pictures. The partners felt that CBC sounded too much like "corned beef and cabbage." Various names were considered, and finally Columbia Pictures Corporation was chosen.

From the beginning, Columbia seemed destined to fare well. It came to life on the single stage on Gower Street and quickly developed into a complete picture-making plant. Within a few years, many of the small independent studios, which were located on Gower Street, Beachwood Drive, and Sunset Boulevard, were acquired by rapidly growing Columbia Pictures.

One of the motion picture production "giants," Twentieth Century-Fox, got its start in 1914 when William Fox filmed *Life's Shop Window* on Staten Island. In December of the following year, a party of Fox players, headed by Winfield Sheehan, left New York to explore the wild and woolly West.

Within a few days after their arrival in Los Angeles, they had completed arrangements for taking over the former Selig Studio at 1845 Allesandro Street, in Edendale, California.

About July 1916, the company began the making of comedies. Because of their great success, five additional comedy companies were quickly

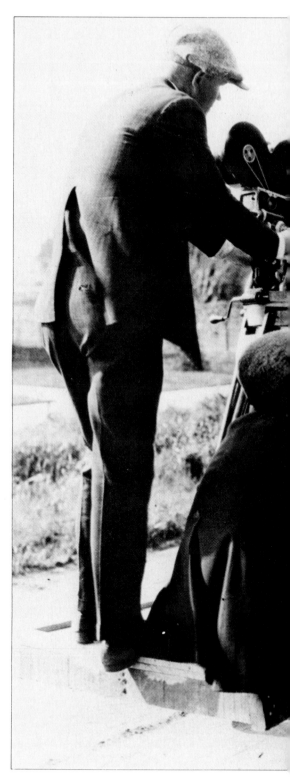

Top: A 1922 aerial photo of the Charles Chaplin domain, which occupied the entire east-side block of La Brea between Sunset and De Longpre; the Chaplin residence [upper left] is now the site of a supermarket; the Chaplin Studio is now the home of A&M Records. Middle: The H. Paulis and William Horsley studios, located on Sunset, just east of Gower; this was the location of many small independent studios that later became known as Poverty Row and [around the corner] Gower Gulch; 1921. Bottom: A 1921 photo of the first buildings and movie sets of the William Fox Studios on Sunset and Western Avenue in Hollywood; in a few years, Fox would become one of the majors in the industry. Right: Comedian Harold Lloyd gets stopped by a motorcycle policeman in a scene for one of his films; from the looks of the sagging, rickety platform built for the camera and cameramen, it was evident that they had to be stuntmen of sorts, too.

added to the list. This continued increase made it obvious that the three-quarters-of-an-acre studio could no longer accommodate the needs of the rapidly expanding motion picture company. Consequently, in late 1916, Fox purchased the former Thomas Dixon Studio, a property of five-and-one-half acres located on the west side of Western Avenue at Sunset Boulevard.

In addition to an old-fashioned frame cottage nestled in a lemon grove, there stood only a large glass-covered stage, a two-story laboratory, and an office building. New equipment and a generating plant were installed and reinforced with such working apparatus as could be moved from the Edendale studio. In addition, new stages and workshops were erected. Production was growing so rapidly that Fox purchased eight additional acres immediately across Western Avenue. The total realty investment for the thirteen and one-half acres was $215,000.

The Fox facility became large enough to have twenty productions shooting at one time and, by 1925, the company turned out eighty-three films. Forty-nine of these were special attractions, while the remainder were comedies. Between 1916 and 1925, Fox spent $15 million to produce 660 films on Western Avenue. Its production schedule grew so heavy that in 1923 the company bought 250 acres of land in the Beverly Hills area, and much of the production moved to what was named the Fox Hills Studio. Fox's corporate headquarters, however, remained on Western Avenue.

One of the greatest contributions to the motion picture industry was made by Harry, Jack, Sam, and Albert Warner. In 1918, the four brothers produced a hit feature called *My Four Years in Germany,* based on a book by Ambassador James W. Gerard. The brothers built a tremendous studio facility, with a colonnaded, neo-Colonial-style administration building, on Sunset Boulevard near Bronson Avenue. Its back lot contained some of the largest shooting stages in the industry. In 1925, Warner Brothers purchased the 25-acre studios of the old Vitagraph Company at Prospect and Tal-

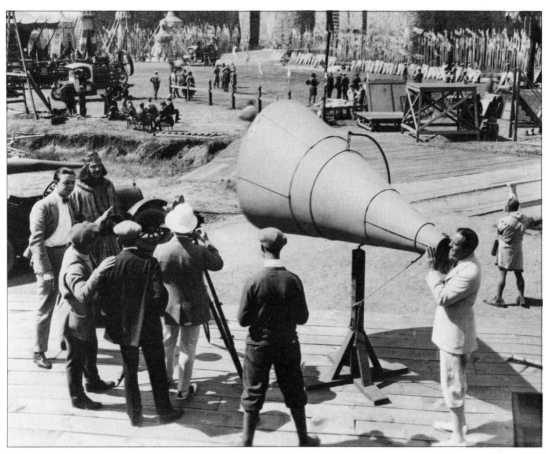

Opposite page: An aerial view of Pickford-Fairbanks Studio, with its enormous *Robin Hood* set. Above: Douglas Fairbanks uses a huge megaphone to communicate with hundreds of extras during the *Robin Hood* filming; such cumbersome devices were necessary before electronically amplified sound was developed.

madge Avenues [now the site of television station KABC].

Warner Brothers' meteoric rise in the movie business was due in large measure to its popular creative talent, including former stage actor John Barrymore, singer Al Jolson, choreographer Busby Berkeley, and a multitalented German shepherd named Rin-Tin-Tin. In 1926, Warner Brothers pioneered synchronized sound in motion pictures, first with music and sound effects in *Don Juan,* and the following year with song and dialogue in *The Jazz Singer*. In 1928, the studio released the first *all-*talking picture, *The Lights of New York*. The brothers changed the entire technology and character of the picture industry, and when they left Hollywood in 1928, after buying out First National Studios on Barham Boulevard in Burbank, their company was considered the leader of the business.

By 1925, the Famous Players-Lasky Corporation studio was feeling the need for more space, so, in 1926, they purchased and moved to the vast United Studios at Marathon Street and Van Ness Avenue. The old studio facility at Sunset Boulevard and Vine street was immediately demolished, except for the old barn used in the making of *The Squaw Man*. The barn was moved to the new studio location where it was used for a variety of purposes. Forty years later, on December 27, 1956, the barn was dedicated California State Landmark No. 554 in ceremonies attended by such movie moguls as Jesse Lasky, Cecil B. DeMille, Adolph Zukor, Frank Freeman, and Samuel Goldwyn.

In 1927, the studio's name was changed to Paramount-Famous-Lasky Corporation and, in 1920, it was again changed—this time to Paramount Publix. Five years later, the name Para-

Top: The cover of a 1926 issue of the *Hollywood News* motion picture section. Bottom: A Hollywood automobile dealer's ad. Right: In 1926, the Famous Players-Lasky Corporation purchased United Studios, on Melrose, and began an immediate expansion and modernization program; here, Lasky [on right] and others watch as an actress pretends to nail the Paramount Avenue street sign.

mount Pictures Incorporated emerged.

By the latter part of the 1920s, almost every motion picture studio that hadn't been bought out had grown into a little corporate principality ruled by an absolute monarch or two, administered by knights wielding typewriters and adding machines, thronged with jesters and magicians, worked by peasants who built sets, hooked up lights, edited film, drove trucks, scribbled scenarios, fell off horses, and pushed pencils so that those outside the magical gates could be entertained.

The Masquers Club

Writers, as well as actors of world renown, were flocking to Hollywood to write scenarios or assist in filming of their books. Having come and found the climate and intellectual atmosphere congenial, they built, bought, or rented homes. Several members of the Screenwriters Guild of the Authors' League of America formed the Writers' Club in 1921 and bought a six-room residence at Sunset

Above: A view of Hollywood High School, 1923. Right, top: A policeman directs traffic at the intersection of Hollywood Boulevard and Cahuenga: this area was the heart of the Wilcox Ranch in 1887, when Harvey Wilcox filed the map first bearing the name Hollywood; this was also the intersection of the Tilting Tournament; 1923. Right, below: The Hollywood Tire Shop; the owner, Vernon Farquhar, is in the foreground; photo taken 1923.

and Las Palmas to use as a clubhouse. The club later took in actors, producers, and directors, and acquired a huge membership. The Writers' Club would eventually evolve into the Writers Guild of America, West, the organization that protects the scriptwriters and their work from unfair practices.

By the mid-1920s, the motion picture business was, unquestionably, the primary industry in Hollywood. However, the actors did not have their own club where they could rendezvous and fraternize with each other. Eight actors, who were transplanted from Broadway in New York, met on April 9, 1925, with a common goal in mind—to form an all-male theatrical club.

The first general meeting and election of officers was held on May 25, and that date became

Barnsdall Park, formerly Olive Hill; 1921.

Workmen at the Union Brick Quarry, Brush canyon; the quarry was at the northern end of Bronson Avenue [1924]; it is now known as the Bronson Caves; the site of many western movies.

the official birthday of The Masquers. "This shall be a theatrical club of love, loyalty, and laughter!" declared Robert Edeson, who became the first harlequin, the name Masquers bestow on their presidents. Then, proposing a toast, he stated: "To the Masquers! We laugh to win." That phrase became the motto of the club, which spent its first two years in a house at Yucca and McCadden Streets. In 1927, Antonio Morino presented the club with an English-style house. Located at 1765 North Sycamore Avenue, it continues to be the home of the famous Masquers.

Valentino

The year after the Masquers Club was organized, the movie world was stunned when it learned of the untimely death of Rudolph Valentino. His funeral in New York was the most heavily attend-

ed in the history of the motion picture business, and his crypt at the Hollywood Cemetery is still visited daily by tourists and fans. Shortly after the death of the famous matinee idol, a campaign was instituted to raise funds for the erection of a monument in his honor. With sufficient funds from subscribers all over the world, sculptor Roger Noble Burnham was commissioned to design and sculpt a statue. After months of work, the magnificent statue was dedicated on the anniversary of Valentino's birth, May 6th, 1930, in DeLongpre Park. Entitled *Aspiration,* the four-foot bronze figure of a nude male, with head stretched to heaven, stands on a beautiful green marble world. Inscribed on the large rectangular base was a fitting tribute to Valentino's popularity.

ERECTED IN MEMORY OF
RUDOLPH VALENTINO
1895-1926
PRESENTED BY HIS FRIENDS AND
ADMIRERS FROM EVERY WALK OF
LIFE IN ALL PARTS OF THE WORLD. IN
APPRECIATION OF THE HAPPINESS BROUGHT
TO THEM BY HIS CINEMA PORTRAYALS.

For many years, on Memorial Day, a "mystery" woman placed a wreath at the foot of the monument. The statue was stolen from its pedestal in the 1950s, but was later recovered. Fearing continued thefts, the city stored the statue in a warehouse until 1976, when it was remounted on its original pedestal.

New Office Buildings and Hotels

Shortly after the motion pictures migrated to Hollywood, the community began to grow out—and up. In the ten years between 1921 and 1931, Hollywood Boulevard sprouted a skyline of new office buildings, apartment houses, and hotels, each with its own unique architectural character. Many of them attained the then-legal height limit of twelve stories.

The office buildings, which established Hollywood for the first time as a desirable location for doctors, lawyers, and other office professionals,

Top: The dedication ceremony for the Hollywoodland sign atop Mt. Lee was held in 1923; the sign was erected by developers as an advertising gimmick, but decades later would become the symbol for revitalizing Hollywood. Bottom: An indication of the sign's size is revealed by this posing construction worker.

were some of the tallest and most imposing of the new structures. They surrounded Hollywood and Vine: the Taft Building [1924], the B.H. Dyas Company [1928—it became the Broadway in 1931], and the Equitable Building [1930]. Other twelve-story towers included the Guaranty Bank Building [1924] at Hollywood and Ivar and the Security First National Bank Building [1928] at Hollywood and Highland. The boulevard also became home to the Hollywood Professional Building [1926], at Sycamore and the Security Trust and Savings Building [1922] at Cahuenga.

Other luxury hotels joined the Hollywood Hotel: the Christie [1923] at Hollywood and McCadden, the Knickerbocker [1925] on Ivar, just north of Hollywood, the Plaza [1925], south of Hollywood and Vine, and the Roosevelt [1927], across the street from Sid Grauman's new Chinese Theatre at Orange Drive.

The demand for high-quality housing resulted in a number of prestigious apartment towers being erected. One of these was the Garden Court Apartments on Hollywood Boulevard, just east of La Brea Avenue. Built in 1919, the magnificent structure of Italian Renaissance design boasted of thick Oriental carpets, baby grand pianos, and fine oil paintings in every apartment. During its heyday, many noted personalities including Louis B. Mayer, Mack Sennett, and Mae Murray called the Garden Court home.

Another prestigious Hollywood address, the Chateau Elysee Apartments, was completed in 1929 by Eleanor Ince, the widow of the pioneer film producer Thomas Ince. The French Normandy-style building consisted of seventy-seven apartments, varying in size from one-bedroom units to deluxe two-story, three-bedroom apartments.

Despite the fact that many of the tenants were permanent residents, the Chateau Elysee was operated like a hotel. The dining room served three meals a day and daily maid service was provided. Room service was available and the switchboard operators screened all calls.

During Mrs. Ince's ownership, some of Holly-wood's most prominent actors and actresses were full- or part-time residents. Many of the entertainers who lived in New York also maintained apartments at the Chateau Elysee, in order to have a comfortable and familiar place to stay when filming in Hollywood. This is where Gable and Lombard lived—and loved. Other stars, including Humphrey Bogart, Edward G. Robinson, Errol Flynn, and Ginger Rogers, lived in opulence and ease.

In 1951, the beautiful building was sold to Fifield Manors, who operated it as a residence for the elderly until 1973, when they sold it to the Church of Scientology.

The Garden Of Allah

One of Hollywood's most famous, or infamous, hotel-apartment complexes was the Garden of Allah at 8150 Sunset Boulevard. Built in 1921 by the popular actress Alla Nazimova, the garden opened with an eighteen-hour party. Entertained by troubadours playing madrigals from the middle of the pool, the celebrity guests were treated to a lavish and stately dinner.

When the Great Depression struck, Alla Nazimova lost every dollar she put into the hotel. After her death in 1945, the Garden of Allah continued as a hotel and sanctuary for many of Hollywood's famed celebrities. In the thirty-two year span of its life, the garden witnessed robbery, murder, drunkenness, despair, divorce, marriages, orgies, pranks, fights, suicides, frustraion, and hope. Yet intellectuals and celebrities from all over the world were to find it a convenient haven and a fascinating home. Among those who frequently stayed at the famous garden were Ramon Navarro, Errol Flynn, F. Scott Fitzgerald, Sheilah Graham, John O'Hara, Robert Benchley, Gilbert Roland, Tallulah Bankhead, Clara Bow, and Leopold Stokowski. It was not uncommon to see tourists and movie fans lining the sidewalk just to get a glimpse of their favorite star.

By the late 1940s, the Garden of Allah had gained such a questionable reputation that many

SOUVENIR-
PROGRAM

PREMIERE

Douglas Fairbanks

"The Thief of Bagdad"

Thursday Evening, July 10th, 1924

D. J. GRAUMAN, Founder   SID GRAUMAN, Managing Director

Grauman's Egyptian
Theatre
Hollywood Boulevard at McCadden Place
HOLLYWOOD, CALIFORNIA

personalities no longer wished to stay there. In addition, it didn't have many of the modern conveniences that the newer and more glamorous hotels possessed. In 1950, after years of operating in the red, the Garden of Allah was sold to Lytton Savings and Loan, who bought it to tear down and build its home office. However, the Garden of Allah did not go without a whimper. It had a last bang. It had opened with a party and it ended with one. Three hundred and fifty guests were invited, but close to a thousand came to impersonate the people who had been glamorous stars when the garden had opened. Francis X. Bushman and his wife, Iva, were the only ones in attendance who were present at the original christening party in 1927. Most of the starlets were scantily dressed, hoping to catch a producer's roving eye. By midnight, the pool was full of empty liquor bottles, reminiscent of the Garden's flamboyant history.

The day after the party, the fixtures and furnishings were sold at public auction, where some of the former residents were among the bidders.

Above: This photo of Grauman's Egyptian Theatre was taken in 1924: Oriental shops line the left side of its forecourt. The Egyptian was the first Grauman theater in Hollywood, and opened with a premiere of Douglas Fairbank's *Robin Hood* in 1922. Still one of Hollywood's finest, the Egyptian has been the site of countless movie premieres, such as the one listed on the program at left.

Actors pose at the entrance to United Studios in 1924. It was formerly the Robert Brunton Studios. United sold out to Famous Players-Lasky in 1926, who later became Paramount Pictures.

Errol Flynn's bed was most sought after. When the wrecker's ball demolished the Garden of Allah, it marked the end to a bit of Hollywood history that can only be found in old movie magazines.

The Hollywood Board of Trade, which had tended to Hollywood's business and service needs from its days as Cahuenga Valley, was no longer large enough to serve the interests of all the community's businessmen after the picture industry electrified the area. In 1921, the Hollywood Chamber of Commerce was formed, with Dr. Allan Shore as its first president. The first home for the new organization was located at 6553 Hollywood Boulevard. In 1923, the chamber relocated to 6530 Hollywood Boulevard, where they stayed until an elaborate new building, located at 6520 Sunset Boulevard, was completed in 1926. This facility more than served its purpose for fifty years, at which time the chamber relocated to 6324 Sunset Boulevard in 1976.

The chamber's first major activity was to form a special committee whose job was to convince all the Hollywood Boulevard merchants to leave their lights on after 9 P.M. Hitherto, Hollywood's boom had manifested itself primarily during the day; it was said one could shoot a cannon down Hollywood Boulevard at 9 P.M. without danger of hitting anything. The merchants complied, and, with the exception of a brief blackout period during the Second World War, the lights stayed on, helping to enhance the boulevard's image as the Great White Way of the West. Large department stores and specialty shops began settling on the boulevard and encouraged small merchants to join them. As shoppers from all over the Los Angeles area came to shop where the stars shop, Hollywood gained the reputation of being the most exclusive shopping district in the West.

Top: William Mulholland speaks to the crowd who are assembled for the dedication ceremony of the Hollywood Lake and Mulholland Dam. The dam is unique in that it's in the center of a large metropolitan area. The official ceremony was held on March 17, 1925; the dam was completed in December 1924, and is constructed of solid concrete, 160 feet thick at its base. At left: workmen put the finishing touches to the Hollywood Lake and Mulholland Dam.

Top: The Woman's Club of Hollywood, Hollywood Boulevard at La Brea, 1924. Bottom: Chaplin Studios on La Brea; the tudor architectural style made it one of the most attractive studios in the city; much of it has been preserved; photo taken 1925.

Santa Claus Lane Parade

The chamber's oldest and certainly most popular activity is the Santa Claus Lane Parade. In 1924, the Retail Merchants Bureau, a division of the Chamber of Commerce, instituted a campaign for increasing the Christmas business of the merchants on Hollywood Boulevard. Street decorations, consisting of imitation fireplace chimneys, were placed on prominent corners. In addition, large papier-mache Santa Claus heads, about four feet in length, and real Christmas trees were mounted on the ornamental light standards. This decoration was varied with bunting and overhead Christmas lights hung over the street. Thus, the name Santa Claus Lane was formally adopted. For years, the property owners, headed by Colonel Harry M. Baine, and the merchants through the Retail Merchants Bureau, and later the Hollywood Merchants Association, continued and enlarged this activity.

In 1928, Colonel Baine, through the use of funds provided by the property owners, initiated a new Christmas activity, which was destined to become one of the outstanding features of the succeeding Christmas seasons. Making arrangements with the Los Angeles County Park Department for their care, he succeeded in acquiring a team of two live reindeer. These animals were stabled on Hollywood Boulevard at La Brea for the constant admiration of the community. For two years, during the month of December, they were driven down the boulevard, pulling a sleigh on wheels and usually carrying, in addition to Santa Claus, a popular entertainment celebrity. The first movie star to travel down Santa Claus Lane with Santa was Jeanette Loff, a Pathe player.

Looking northwest at the Hollywoodland subdivision and sales office, at the northern end of Beachwood Drive. Photo, 1924.

For some unknown reason, Santa did not travel down Santa Claus Lane in 1930. However, on December 12, 1931, this practice was resumed, much to the delight of the Hollywood residents and the many children who traveled to see Santa. Instead of using real reindeer to pull the sleigh, the Otto K. Olesen Illuminating Company mounted a sleigh and four model reindeer on a flat trailer, which was pulled with a truck. As the float made its way down Hollywood Boulevard, a machine sprayed artificial snow flakes over the float, there-

by creating the illusion of a snow storm.

In 1932, the Otto K. Olesen Illuminating Company designed a new Santa Claus Christmas float, which had its debut when it appeared in the first Santa Claus Lane Parade held on December 10, 1932. Sponsored by the Hollywood Merchants Association, and witnessed by thousands of spectators, the parade started at Vine Street and traveled west on Hollywood Boulevard to La Brea Avenue. In addition to the Santa Claus float, the

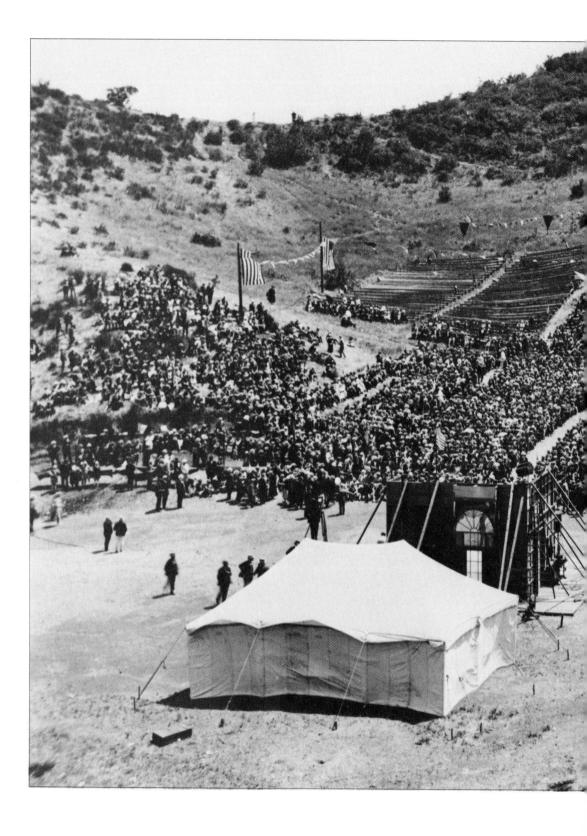

A performance at the Hollywood Bowl, 1922.

Above: The completion and dedication ceremonies for the new Hollywood Post Office at 1717 Vine Street [1925]; when the post office moved, the building became a cafeteria—next to the Palace—and today stands vacant. Left: The classic lines of Doric architecture give a feeling of strength and permanency to the Hollywood Masonic Temple on Hollywood Boulevard. The building was completed in 1922 at a cost of $250,000; photo taken 1925.

Easter Sunrise Services at the Hollywood Bowl, 1925, a Bowl tradition since 1921; the cross is formed by the choir children.

first parade consisted of a color guard, drum and bugle corps, and marchers from American Legion Post 43. Accompanying Santa Claus on his trip down Santa Claus Lane were the popular film stars Gloria Stuart and Lawrence Grant.

The year 1932 also saw the installation of metal Christmas trees that lined Hollywood Boulevard. Each tree was sixteen-feet high, contained 160 lights and weighed 750 pounds.

Because of the overwhelming response to the first pageant, the 1933 parade was greatly expanded to include bands, motion picture personalities, equestrian teams, and city and county officials. Just before the parade began, actress Patricia Ellis pulled the electrical switch to light the trees and decorations that lined Santa Claus Lane. Each night after the parade, until Christmas, Santa Claus and his float drove down Santa Claus Lane, accompanied by personalities such as Noah Beery, Rita La Roy, and Patricia Ellis.

For the next eight years, the parade included

many of Hollywood's most popular celebrities, including Mary Pickford, Bette Davis, Kent Taylor, Andy Devine, Dorothy Lamour, Wallace Beery, Rudy Vallee, Tom Mix, Monte Montana, George Burns, Gracie Allen, Bob Hope, Basil Rathbone, Fanny Brice, and Bing Crosby. During World War II [1942, 1943, and 1944], the parade was discontinued. To aid in the war effort, the Hollywood Chamber of Commerce donated the metal Santa Claus Lane Christmas trees to Uncle Sam and replaced them with large papier-mache Santa Claus heads.

When the war was over in 1945, the parade was resumed on November 23, with a record crowd of onlookers. During the succeeding years, the Santa Claus Lane Parade developed into one of the most spectacular parades in the country. With the cooperation of the community, the Hollywood Chamber of Commerce, and participating motion

Top: California Studios [with the dome of its stage visible in the background] and Bischoff, Inc. were two of the many independent studios on Gower, south of Sunset, that occupied the area known as Poverty Row; this site is now occupied by the Sunset-Gower Studios [formerly Columbia]; photo 1925. Right: Independent Pictures Corporation was another of the Poverty Row group, which included Russell Productions, H. Paulis, and Wilnat Productions—all of whom lasted only a few months; 1925.

picture personalities, the parade has grown in size to include more than three hundred separate entries. Marching bands, equestrian groups, entertainment celebrities, and others come from all over the country to participate in this world-renowned parade, which is viewed by thousands in person, and millions through the magic of television.

Service Clubs

During the early Twenties, three business-men's service clubs were organized. The Lions Club of Hollywood was chartered in February 1923, only a jump ahead of the Kiwanis Club, which received its charter that May. Hollywood Rotary International was chartered in March 1925.

The Lions' first project was to furnish the new Hollywood Hospital, Hollywood's first adult hospital [Children's Hospital was built at Vermont and Sunset in 1920]. The hospital had been conceived when a Hollywood Hotel guest became too ill to be moved to the nearest hospital in Los Angeles;

Left: The Hollywood Legion Stadium was located on El Centro, just south of Hollywood Boulevard; managed by the Hollywood Chapter of the American Legion, the stadium was a mecca for weekly boxing matches; photo 1926. Below: The Outpost Estates sales office on the northwest corner of Franklin Avenue and Outpost Drive; this subdivision was one of the most exclusive in Hollywood, and today is home for many famous and prominent citizens; 1926.

the house physician had to find him a bed in what was a local insane asylum. By 1922, hotel owner Mira Hershey had organized the Hollywood Hospital Company. The new hospital was built at 1322 Vermont Avenue, just south of Children's Hospital. When it was completed in 1924, the Lions Club raised $100,000 to furnish the hospital.

The Kiwanis Club created a scholarship program for Hollywood High School students and a dental clinic at the Los Angeles Orphans Home among its first projects. Hollywood Rotary sponsored the Crippled Children, the Boy Scouts, and the YMCA in its early years.

Shortly after World War I, one of Hollywood's most charitable organizations, The Assistance League of Southern California, was founded by Mrs. Hancock Banning. Upon establishing its clubhouse at DeLongpre and St. Andrews avenues, the league started a day nursery for children whose mothers worked in the early film studios. In 1929, the Assistance League founded its girls club, which over the years taught its members everything from cooking to gymnastics.

Having had enormous success with the girls club, the league formed the Boys Club of Hollywood in 1937. They took ten boys under their

Sight-seers pose for the photographer before boarding their "Parlor Car" bus for a tour of Hollywood in 1926. Opposite page: Hundreds of movie fans gather in the forecourt of Graumans Egyptian Theater for a glimpse of the stars who will be attending the gala, twin-bill "Doug and Mary Premiere," which featured *Sparrows*, starring Mary Pickford and *Black Pirate*, starring Douglas Fairbanks; 1926.

wing and converted a garage on their property into a clubhouse.

As the membership increased, so did the need for a larger and more complete clubhouse. Property was acquired at 5619 DeLongpre Avenue and, with donated materials and labor, the new facility was dedicated in 1945. By this time, the membership had grown to 500 boys. Activities included recreational coaching, cultural education, guidance, and conseling.

Membership continued to swell, thereby causing the board of directors to embark on a building fund campaign headed by comedian Bob Hope. After raising more than $200,000, a gymnasium and swimming pool became welcomed additions to the program. Today, the Boys Club of Hollywood is a separate corporation from the league, and serves the needs of approximately eighteen hundred boys, who avail themselves of a wide variety of recreational and cultural programs.

Newspapers

Two years after the Assistance League was formed, Harlan Palmer changed the name of his *Hollywood Citizen* newspaper to the *Hollywood Daily Citizen*. In 1921, F.W. Kellogg began issuing another newspaper, *The Hollywood News*. Three years later, the paper was sold to Colonel Ira Copley to add to his string of newspapers, which in rural communities pretty much encircled Los Angeles.

In 1931, *The Hollywood News* was purchased by Harlan Palmer, who combined it with his *Hollywood*

Daily Citizen to create the *Hollywood Citizen News*. In 1948, the newspaper dropped the name Hollywood and continued operating as the *Citizen News*. After Harlan Palmer's death in 1956, his son, Harlan Palmer Jr., took over the reins as publisher of the popular newspaper. Over the next few years, it became the fourth largest daily newspaper in Los Angeles.

The Trade Papers

While the *Citizen News* was of general circulation, the motion picture industry did not have its own newspaper. This was remedied in 1930 when W.R. Wilkerson founded the first daily trade paper. After finding a financial backer, he put the first issue of *The Hollywood Reporter* on the streets on September 3, 1930. Three years later, almost to the day, the second daily trade paper was born. Founded by Sime Silverman, who also founded *Variety* in 1905, the first issue of *Daily Variety* was published on September 6, 1933. Both trade papers were warmly welcomed by the motion picture industry, causing them to be enviable successes. Today, both trades enjoy national and international circulation, with subscribers who read them religiously.

Beth-El and Temple Israel

Until 1921, Hollywood's Jewish population was forced to worship outside the boundaries of Hollywood for lack of a temple. That year, several

prominent Jewish citizens met to discuss their religious needs, and, as a result, Hollywood's first synagogue, Beth-El, was organized on January 26, 1922. A few months later, a lot was purchased for $8,500 at 1508 North Wilton Place and plans for the erection of a temple were underway. The fundraising slogan adopted in 1922 also served as a time schedule, "For All To See In '23." In September of that year, services for the High Holy Days were held in their new building, even though the interior was unfinished. Years later, property was purchased on Crescent Heights Boulevard, where a beautiful new synagogue was erected to house the growing congregation.

Hollywood's second Jewish temple, the Temple Israel, was conceived in 1925, at the Fox Studios—In the office of Sol M. Wurtzel, the temple's first president. After using a private residence and another church as their temporary synagogue, the congregation built a magnificent temple at 7300 Hollywood Boulevard.

During the time the community's Jewish population was establishing its two houses of worship, the citizens of Hollywood were informed, in 1922, that the lower part of Weid Canyon had been purchased for the purpose of building a dam. The Chamber of Commerce formed a dam committee to investigate the matter. Concerned for the safety of the residents and property owners in the event

Top: The Garden Court Apartments, 1926; in its day, the Garden Court was one of the finest apartment buildings in the city, with original paintings, Oriental rugs, and a grand piano in every suite; Louis B. Mayer and his wife, Margaret, were among the many prominent people who have lived there; it remains standing today, on Hollywood near Sycamore Avenue, impressive even in sad repair. Bottom: UniJentified employees of the Jack White production group pose before a billboard. Mermaid Comedies were among the most successful films of the 1920s.

the proposed dam ruptured, the committe met with the chief engineer, William Mulholland, to air their grievances. After several meetings with the distinguished engineer, the committe was finally convinced that the dam posed no threat to the citizens of Hollywood.

Work was started in August of 1923, with

Above: Students and faculty of the Misses Janes School on Hollywood Boulevard, east of Whitley; the private school catered to the children of stars and prominent citizens, and closed the year this photo was taken [1926]; the Janes home is the only private residence still standing on Hollywood Boulevard between Vermont and La Brea. Left: The Hollywood Chamber of Commerce Building on Sunset; this was the chamber's home for fifty years, and is still standing; 1926.

Saturday Night

TEN CENTS A COPY $5 A YEAR BY MAIL

Vol. 6. No. 23   LOS ANGELES, CALIFORNIA   April 17, 1926

Hollywood's New Legitimate Theater, El Capitan

UNDER MANAGEMENT OF EDWARD D. SMITH, LESSEE, WILL OPEN MONDAY, MAY 3, WITH THE CHARLOT REVUE

—For Description See Next Page

HOLLYWOOD
MAGAZINE
Formerly HOLLY LEAVES
By Mail Every Friday

Entered as second class matter, June 18, 1925, at the postoffice at Los Angeles, Cal., under the Act of March 3, 1879

TWO QUEENS AND AN ACE—Here is the trio who will star at the El Capitan inauguration and all the time afterwards. They are, left to right, Beatrice Lillie, Jack Buchanan and Gertrude Lawrence. They make their bow to Hollywood and Los Angeles Monday night next in "Charlot's Revue."

1645 Cherokee Ave.
Hollywood, Cal.

10 Cents per Copy
$2.00 per Year

Vol. 15. No. 16

Friday, April 30, 1926

Two periodicals of the day hearld the opening of the El Capitan, known today as the Paramount Theater.

Opposite page: Horse-drawn graders excavate
for the new Hollywood Bowl, 1926. Above:
The first Frank Lloyd Wright-designed
shell at the Bowl, using material from
the sets of *Robin Hood*, donated by
the Pickford-Fairbanks Studios; 1927 photo.
Left: Indians camp on the grounds
of the Bowl for an Indian conclave held in
Southern California in September of 1927.

Mulholland supervising the construction. When the work was completed in December of 1924 [dedication ceremonies were held on March 17, 1925], the new Mulholland Dam stood 200 feet high and was characterized by engineers from every section of the country as possessing one of the most beautiful architectural designs of any dam in America. Mulholland Dam created Hollywood Lake, which has supplied Hollywood with most of its water for more than fifty years.

The Chinese and Other Theaters

By the early Twenties, enormous, ornate theaters, known as movie palaces, had been built in San Francisco and Los Angeles. Between 1922 and 1930, Hollywood was to share in this wealth of palaces, with the construction of four of the most beautiful theaters in the country. The first of these, Grauman's Egyptian Theatre, was followed by the Grauman's Chinese Theater, Warner Brothers Theater, and finally, the Hollywood Pantages. Each one was both larger and more ornate than the previous.

For several years, C.E. Toberman had attempted to induce Sid Grauman and his father to locate in Hollywood. The two Graumans had come to Los Angeles and built the lavish Million Dollar Theater at Third and Broadway. When Grauman finally agreed in 1922, Toberman built the huge Egyptian Theater on Hollywood Boulevard east of McCadden Place. It was named the year the discovery of King Tutankhamen's tomb created an instant society of Egyptologists.

The theater featured a long courtyard entry designed to resemble an Egyptian temple and lined with potted plants and ornate murals. Inside the auditorium, carved columns and sphinxes flanked the stage. The opening feature was *Robin Hood*, the first of a fifty-year string of gala premieres, complete with searchlights, limousines, and autograph-hunting fans, that the Egyptian Theatre would host.

With the Egyptian Theatre experiencing immense success, Sid Grauman was looking to build another theater. He again contacted Toberman, who secured a long-term lease on property located at 6925 Hollywood Boulevard. By 1925, the firm of Meyer & Holler had completed the plans for Grauman's Chinese Theatre. It was planned to make it a veritable museum of the Chinese arts, architecture, and culture. Official government authorization was gained for the importation of temple bells, pagodas, Fu Dogs, and rare artifacts.

On Armistice Day, November 11, 1925, the first rivet in the steel girders was driven by the beautiful Chinese actress Anna May Wong. During the course of construction, an accident occurred that later evolved to one of Hollywood's greatest tourist attractions: the placing of celebrities' hand and footprints in the forecourt of the Chinese Theater. There have been many stories as to the origin of the tradition, and all can be dismissed as folklore. The most popular of the fabricated tales suggests that the idea for the hand and footprints was sparked when Sid Grauman witnessed Norma Talmadge step into fresh cement as she got out of her car while visiting the theater. It has also been the popular belief that Norma Talmadge was the first celebrity to place hand and footprints in the theater's forecourt. The true story, which lacks the glamour of the other tales, is that Sid Grauman was walking across the theater's forecourt when he was confronted by his chief cement mason, Jean Klossner, who scolded Sid for walking in the freshly laid cement. After making peace with Klossner, Sid asked Douglas Fairbanks, Mary Pickford, and Norma Talmadge to come to the theater at once. Upon their arrival, he had them place their footprints in the new curbstone. However, the cement was nearly dry, causing the impressions to be too faint. In April, just three weeks before the completion of construction, Mary Pickford and Douglas Fairbanks were again invited back—this time to formally place their hand and footprints and signatures in the center of the theater's forecourt. A few days later, Grauman had Norma Talmadge make similar impressions next to those made by Pickford and Fairbanks. Knowing that the theater's grand opening was to occur on May 18, 1927, Norma Talmadge scribbled that date above her signature instead of the date she actually made the impressions. Since then, scores of celebrities have had their hand and footprints and signatures enshrined in the famous courtyard.

The theater had its grand opening on May 18, 1927, when Cecil B. DeMille's *King of Kings* was premiered. Hundreds of fans thronged the streets outside the theater to view the magnificent structure and to seek the autographs from the arriving stars dripping with mink and diamonds in the best Hollywood tradition. It was written in the papers as the grandest opening ever held.

The grandeur of the building was far beyond the public's imagination. With a magnificently carved ceiling, muraled walls, plush carpeting and ornate columns, it was by far one of the most beautiful theaters in the world.

The Chinese Theatre has hosted more premieres than any other theater in Hollywood. Opening nights are attended in rich measure by stars, producers, writers, and technicians. Their presence easily makes a Hollywood premiere the most glamorous and exciting spectacle in the field of entertainment.

The third of the grand Hollywood theaters was the Warner Brothers Theater situated on the north corner of Hollywood Boulevard and Wilcox Avenue. The brothers Warner, who had been extremely successful at making movies, decided to get into the business of showing films. After fourteen months of construction, the Warner Brothers Theater opened amid great fanfare on the evening of April 26, 1928. The event was also the premiere of *Glorious Betsy*, starring Delores Costello and Conrad Nagle. Typical of all premieres, it was attended by Hollywood's finest. The theater seated over 2,700 people, and was at that time the largest theater in Hollywood. Behind the great murals on either side of the auditorium were the chambers that housed the twenty-six ranks of the four-manual Marr & Colton pipe organ. It was one of the few theaters large enough to convert to Cinerama in 1952. A giant new semicircular screen curved into the auditorium and three new projection booths were built to accommodate the three synchronized projectors required for early Cinerama. The theater is now called the Hollywood Pacific, renamed when that chain purchased it in 1968.

The last of Hollywood's great movie palaces was opened on the evening of June 4, 1930. The long-awaited opening was for its newest, largest [seating capacity of 2,812], most original, and certainly most ornate theater—The Hollywood Pantages. The theater, located on Hollywood Boulevard just east of Vine Street and designed by B. Marcus Priteca, was the last to bear the name of its founder, Alexander Pantages.

The opening attraction was the world premiere of *Floradora Girl*, starring Marion Davies. The invited guests—practically every movie star in Hollywood—stepped from their limousines onto a red velvet-carpeted sidewalk and saw, for the first time, the lavish marble and bronze entrance lit from the elaborate 18-foot ceiling by hundreds of tiny bulbs.

Of all of the theaters in Hollywood, the Pantages was, by far, the grandest. The vaulted grand lobby, the largest in Los Angeles, was flanked by

Left: Hollywood & Vine,
when it was just another
intersection [1927];
this view is of the northeast
corner, now occupied
by the Equitable Building;
the used car lot is
now the site of the
Pantages Theater. Above:
Looking west down Hollywood
Boulevard from Vine;
the palms are in the front
yard of a private residence.
This photo was taken in 1927.

twin stairways at either end and covered by the most original modern ceiling in gold and henna shades. The auditorium was both awesome and breathtaking. The stage, also the largest in Los Angeles except for the Shrine Auditorium, was 70-feet wide and 180-feet long.

Like the other major Hollywood theaters, premieres were held continuously at the Pantages. In 1949, when RKO acquired the theater, the Academy Awards moved in and the gala event was held there annually for ten years.

As commercial properties blossomed in downtown Hollywood, subdividers carved the hills and former orange groves into valuable residential lots. Oilman G. Allen Hancock, who owned most of the land to Hollywood's immediate south, between Melrose and Wilshire, decided there was even more money in real estate than there was in oil. The oil derricks that had studded the old Rancho La Brea for thirty years began to come down, and subdivision of the area began in 1919. By 1925, thirteen tracts, most of them including large lots for impressive homes, formed the core of Hancock Park. Hancock also leased land in the area for the Wilshire Country Club, which opened in December 1920.

Hancock was also instrumental in the formation of the prestigious Los Angeles Tennis Club, when he granted an option for five and one-half acres to the club's organizers in the early Twenties. A few years after two exhibition courts were built on Melrose Avenue, the club built a $50,000 clubhouse and several courts at 5851 Clinton Avenue.

In 1927, the year of the first Pacific Southwest Tournament, additional courts were built in the rear property, bringing the total number to seventeen, plus three practice courts.

The proximity of Hollywood generated a glamorous aura at the club. Regular Southwest boxholders included such personalities as Clark Gable and Carole Lombard, Marlene Dietrich, Myrna Loy, Fred Astaire, William Powell, Charlton Heston, Charles Chaplin, and Janet Gaynor.

Another recreational organization came into existence in the Twenties, when the Hollywood

Above: Contrary to folklore, Norma Talmadge wasn't the first to place her prints and inscribe her name in the wet cement of the Grauman's Chinese forecourt; that distinction goes to Mary Pickford and Douglas Fairbanks; here the duo are shown practicing the feat with Sid Grauman; Fairbanks finally used the wet cement block shown, but Mary put her prints and name in a different block [1927]. Right: The Roosevelt Hotel, just after its opening in 1927; the Cinegrill was added later, and was recently removed when the Roosevelt underwent renovation.

Athletic Club building was completed in 1923. Located at Sunset and Hudson Avenue, it housed a 25-yard swimming pool, a gymnasium, guest rooms, a barbershop, and a full range of extras catering to the well-bred athlete. By 1926, the club boasted 1,000 members and sponsored teams in a dozen sports. For more than thirty years, the Hollywood Athletic Club had been the inspiration and medium for physical development of its members and the home for numerous service clubs and civic organizations responsible for the development of Hollywood.

Hollywoodland

Movie publicists had nothing on land promoters when it came to hoopla and bright lights. The Hollywoodland subdivision syndicate created

one of history's most spectacular—and lengthy—promotion campaigns, and gave the community its most conspicuous landmark.

The subdivision took in 500 acres of wooded canyons and knolls overlooking the business area of Hollywood. To attract attention to the home sites, Harry Chandler, one of the builders, put up a $21,000 sign with letters 50 feet high reading HOLLYWOODLAND on the side of Mt. Cahuenga above the tract.

The letters, about 30 feet wide and nearly 50 feet tall, were composed of 3 x 9-foot sheet metal panels painted white, and were attached to a framework of pipes, wires, scaffolding, and telephone poles dragged up the steep hillsides by caterpillar tractors. A small white dot was also constructed a couple of hundred feet below the sign. An advertising eyecatcher, it consisted of a circular 35-foot diameter sheet metal sign painted white, with twenty-watt lights around the perimeter.

The thirteen-letter sign was studded with four thousand twenty-watt light bulbs spaced every eight inches around the perimeter of each letter and were changed, when they burned out, by Albert Kothe. At night, the brilliant sight could be seen for miles, attracting countless tourists and local residents. It became a prop for some of the scenes in early movies, and aircraft pilots regarded it as a navigational landmark.

To many, Hollywood signified the highest hopes, the ultimate attainment. But to Lillian Millicent "Peg" Entwhistle, noted stage actress and graduate of the world-famous Theater Guild, it spelled only shattered hopes—defeat—despair. She had come to Hollywood to repeat in films her great success on the New York stage, but misfortune and trouble haunted her steps, and, in September 1932, she climbed to the top of the glittering letter "H" that had grimly mocked her for months and jumped to her death fifty feet below.

In 1939, fifteen years after it was built, maintenance of the sign was discontinued. All four thousand light bulbs were stolen. The sign was vandalized and holes appeared in the letters where the sheet metal panels blew off or were removed.

Top: The Writers' Club, which was located at 6700 Sunset, was a haven for many of Hollywood's best writers [1928]. Bottom: The Vine Street Theatre [1928] was one of Hollywood's finest legitimate theaters; in the 30s, it became the CBS Playhouse Theater, from which radio programs were broadcast, including *The Lux Radio Theater*, with host Cecil B. DeMille; in 1954, the theater went legitimate again, becoming the Huntington Hartford Theatre, the name it bears today. Left: Grauman's idea was a stroke of genius, and he knew it; here he is shown helping Norma Shearer leave her impressions in filmdom's history [1927].

In 1945, the development company donated the sign and several hundred adjoining acres to the city's Recreational and Parks Department. Four years later, the sign survived a major crisis. A windstorm blew down the "H," and some nearby residents argued that the sign was a hazard and an eyesore.

The parks' commission decided to tear down the sign, but later reversed itself and allowed the Hollywood Chamber of Commerce to repair the first nine letters and remove the last four. Since

then, the sign has read HOLLYWOOD.

One of the most successful Hollywood subdivisions was C.E. Toberman's Outpost Estates [1924]. Located east of the northern end of La Brea Avenue, it featured a wide variety of lots priced from $3,500 to $50,000. It was an up-to-date tract, with ornamental street lights, concrete roads and sidewalks, and all underground utilities [the last word in modern planning]. The Popular California-Spanish architecture of the day was encouraged, as all houses were required to have tile roofs and plastered walls. This design not only provided a visual harmony throughout the subdivision, but also gave homeowners a measure of protection from the raging brush fires that occasionally swept through the hills.

The movie industry only told half the story of Hollywood's boom years, the same years of prosperity that America enjoyed between Armistice Day and the stock market crash. The real estate dealers had the real scoop on the area. In 1907, the

Above: In 1925, the Vitagraph Company was purchased by Warner Brothers and renamed Warner Brothers-Vitaphone, shown here on Prospect Avenue; the American Broadcasting Company purchased the lot in 1948 and converted it to TV; it is now known as the ABC Television Center. Right: A publicity stunt, 1928 style; Buick dealer Phil Hall arranged to have actor Edward Everett Horton's new convertible delivered directly to his fourth-floor suite at the Hollywood Plaza on Vine Street.

Hollywood area had only twenty-eight real estate brokers. In 1913, two years after the first movie studios arrived, there were fourty-seven. Fifteen years later, Hollywood listed 408 real estate brokers—one for every 370 Hollywood residents. There was gold in them thar hills, all right—and in them thar flats, too.

It took Hollywood some time to catch up with its new infusions of money and residents. It was low on the cultural and recreational attractions considered *de rigueur* for a community of its new size and prestige. Prominent Hollywood citizens took up the cry for local pleasure domes after the war. Some remain today; others failed to outlive their generation.

Above: The first Santa Claus Lane float; Colonel Harry Baine poses with actress Lili Damita; Ora Matthess holds the reindeer; although Lily Damita was scheduled, actress Jeanette Loff was the first movie personality to travel down Santa Claus Lane with Santa Claus; 1928. Right: Holiday season in Hollywood; 1928.

Pleasure Domes

Hollywood Legion Stadium arrived first, built on the site of a proposed prewar armory near the corner of Hollywood and El Centro. The Hollywood Post of the American Legion, which was organized in 1919, bought the property and constructed an outdoor boxing arena with wooden bleachers in 1922. The next year, the legionnaires enclosed and heated the arena.

The richest boxing audience in the world came to watch the Friday-night fights. Spectators regularly filled the arena's 6,000 seats, as eager to watch the stars as the fighters. The Ritz Brothers or the Marx Brothers were usually on hand, climbing into the ring and clowning with the boxers. Mae West was a boxing fan; she would sometimes give wrist watches to the fighters she liked. Charlie

Chaplin would study the boxers' techniques and adapt them to his own screen work. Al Jolson, part owner of world welterweight champion Henry Armstrong, and his wife, Ruby Keeler, were front-row regulars.

Richard Barthelmess, Douglas Fairbanks, Lupe Velez, Rudolph Valentino, Humphrey Bogart, Jean Harlow, Clark Gable, Wallace Beery, Errol Flynn, Lou Costello, the Three Stooges, and Claudette Colbert were also boxing aficionados throughout the arena's career. Stadium regulars included bootleggers, gangsters and gamblers.

Mrs. Christine Witherill Stevenson operated on a somewhat higher plane. Heiress to the Pittsburgh Paint fortune, she arrived in Hollywood in 1918 with the idea of bringing culture to the community by presenting religious plays. In 1919, she established the Theater Arts Alliance with several other leading citizens and set out to find a Hollywood location suitable for the presentation of outdoor theatrical performances. The site chosen was

The Warner Brothers Theatre on Hollywood and Wilcox, shortly after its completion in 1928. Right: The original location of the Musso & Frank Grill, at 6669 Hollywood Boulevard; established in 1919, it is Hollywood's oldest restaurant, and is considered by many to be its finest; in 1936, the restaurant was relocated to larger quarters next door, at 6667, where it has remained; this photo was taken in 1928.

The Wetherby-Kayser Shoe Company on Hollywood Blvd.; 1928.

the property that now contains the Hollywood Bowl; it then bore the euphonious name of Daisy Dell. With the aid of C.E. Toberman, Mrs. Stevenson and fellow alliance member Mrs. Chauncey Clarke purchased the property, valued at $49,000, in September 1919.

The alliance tested the dell's acoustics by setting up a rough platform in the sage brush, dragging a grand piano up the hill, and inviting a prominent local contralto to sing to the field mice. The natural acoustics were perfect.

Mrs. Stevenson engaged San Francisco architect Louis C. Mullgardt to design an outdoor theater. She was pleased with Mullgardt's plans, but the alliance was not—nor did they care for the projected million-dollar cost. They balked when Mrs. Stevenson insisted that they raise an immediate $200,000, and threatened to sell the property to a subdivider if they did not comply.

Five of the eight alliance directors voted to sell the property, but Toberman pointed out that the property had been purchased with the condition that it be used only for civic or cultural purposes, not for personal or corporate gain; it could only be used for the purpose for which it had been bought.

In 1920, the Theater Arts Alliance was dissolved and replaced by the Community Park and Art Association, who acquired title to Daisy Dell.

Performances, under the supervision of Artie Mason Carter, had already begun in the dell, with audiences standing in knee-high weeds and grass, after climbing up the one narrow path leading into the site. The dell got its current name in 1920 when Hugo Kirchhofer, conducting Lionel Barry-

more and the Hollywood Community Chorus in "The Landing of the Pilgrims," exclaimed, "It's like a big bowl—Hollywood Bowl."

The bowl's first Easter Sunrise Service was held March 21, 1921, with W.A. Clark Jr.'s Philharmonic Orchestra playing from a crude plank platform. The service was such a success that Mrs. Carter, who was a member of the reorganized governing body, urged the new directors to approve a series of summer concerts at twenty-five cents per ticket. The association's membership, which numbered about 1,000, sold 36,000 tickets in advance of the first season, raising $9,000.

In anticipation of an actual concert season, physical improvements were made in the bowl. The brush was cleared and some rough grading was done on the amphitheater. Long wooden benches were installed. In August 1921, the first concerts got underway, with Professor Antonio Sarsi conducting the Los Angeles Municipal Symphonic Band. They were a hit.

In 1923, the season was extended to eight weeks and the series renamed "Symphonies Under

Opposite page: The First Presbyterian Church at Carlos and Gower streets [1929]. Above: Modern fire-fighting equipment is displayed in front of the Hollywood Fire Department and police station on Cahuenga near Hollywood Boulevard; 1928.

the Stars." Although admission was held to twenty-five cents per ticket, the bowl was out of debt in 1924. That year, the Community Park and Art Association was reincorporated under the name of Hollywood Bowl Association, and the property was deeded to the County Board of Supervisors in October.

In 1926, the Hollywood Bowl Association began a huge development project to improve the amphitheater and performance space. It took 4,000 sticks of dynamite, 100 kegs of blasting powder, and gangs of mule teams grading out 36,000 yards of dirt to make the bowl symmetrical. The seating area was expanded to three acres, enough to accommodate 17,000 people. A concrete stage 138 feet wide and 90 feet deep was built, with dressing rooms and storage space underneath, and a parking lot was added in back of the stage.

The Hollywood Bowl's first shell, erected in 1922, was nothing more than a large canopy that

Above: The northeast corner of Selma and Cahuenga avenues in 1930. Right, top: The west side of Vine Street, between Sunset and Selma, 1928. Right, bottom: Warner Brothers West Coast studio, at 5842 Sunset Boulevard; today it's radio station KMPC. Opposite page: The 1927 Old Settlers' Day Parade; the horses and surrey depict the principal means of transportation that C.E. "Mr. Hollywood" Toberman utilized twenty years earlier to sell Hollywood Boulevard property at $30 per front foot.

**Grauman's Chinese Theater [1930], featuring Howard Hughes'
RKO production *Hell's Angels*; Sid Grauman's publicity flare
is evidenced by the airplane suspended above the forecourt.**

covered the wood plank stage. It remained until
1926, when the bowl was remodeled and a new
shell erected. This shell was thin at the top, thick at
the sides, and was adorned with oil paintings of
ships on its face. The following year, the bowl
commissioned Lloyd Wright, Jr. to design a new
shell, which was later constructed in ten days,
using lumber and plasterboard from the geometric
design, to resemble a pyramid, with the center
carved out to cover the orchestra. It was used for
the 1927 season, but because it was unattractive,
he was asked to design another shell to be ready
for the 1928 season. Wright designed a new shell
that was made of concentric one-half rings and cost
$7,389 to construct. It was used for the entire 1928
season; however, there was much concern over the
safety of this shell, due to improper construction
and weathering. In March of 1929, plans were
presented for an all-steel shell with dressing rooms
and an instrument room, which would cost $35,000
including architects and engineer's fees. After three

months of construction, the shell was completed
by the opening of the 1929 season, and has been
used ever since.

When Mrs. Christine Witherill Stevenson
withdrew from the Hollywood Bowl in 1920, she
was intent in promoting her religious plays. She
purchased a 29-acre canyon across the Cahuenga
Pass from the Hollywood Bowl. After building a
crude structure, which was later to develop into
the beautiful Pilgrimage Play Theater, Mrs. Stevenson journeyed to the Holy Land to obtain authentic
fabric, utensils, and props. She wrote the entire
play from her translation of the four Gospels according to the King James version of the Bible. The
first performance of the Pilgrimage Play was held
on June 27, 1920, with Henry Herbert starring as
Jesus of Nazareth. Performances were given every
summer in the original structure, until it was destroyed by fire on October 24, 1929. A new the-

Above: Fans line the boulevard at Grauman's
Chinese during the gala premiere
of *Morocco*, starring Marlene
Dietrich. Left: "Aspiration,"
Rudolph Valentino's memorial statue,
which is located in Paul De Longpre Park,
at De Longpre and Cherokee avenues [1930].

Above: The Greek Theatre, shortly after its completion [1930]. Opposite page, top: One of the hottest spots in the 20s was Eddie Brandstatter's Montmartre Cafe, on the second floor of the C.E. Toberman Building at 6757 Hollywood Boulevard; the supper club featured entertainment, dancing, and fine cuisine, and was frequented by filmdom's elite; photo, 1930. Bottom: The interior of the Montmartre [1930]; it was here that such promising newcomers as Al Rinker, Harry Barris, and a fellow named Bing Crosby [The Rhythm Boys] performed; the Montmartre was the first club to offer them work after they left the Paul Whiteman Band and returned to the west coast in 1930.

ater, with seating capacity of 1,312 was built of concrete in ancient Judean architecture and the play reopened in 1931. It continued until 1940, when war conditions caused brief interruptions. During the war, the dressing room sections were converted into dormitories, where hundreds of servicemen slept during visits to Hollywood.

The play was continued after the war and continued until the last performance in 1964. Renamed the John Anson Ford County Cultural Arts Theater in commemoration of Ford's twenty-four year service as County Supervisor of the Third District of Los Angeles, the theater now houses the Los Angeles Shakespeare Festival.

When Mrs. Christine W. Stevenson passed away in 1922, Hollywood was stunned. As a memorial to this fine lady, four of Hollywood's residents caused a 40-foot lighted cross to be erected atop a hill alongside the Pilgrimage Theater. Dedicated on July 8, 1923, the cross, which was built of structural steel and covered with concrete, was the joint effort of George L. Eastman and C.E. Toberman, who furnished the materials and labor,

and of William Lee Woollett, who made the design. The fourth donor was Mrs. Chauncey Clark, who donated the 1,800 incandescent light bulbs used to outline the beautiful cross. In the beginning, Sunday School children assisted in paying for the lighting of the cross, however, this responsibility was later assumed by the Southern California Edison Company. For many years, the cross was kept lighted only at Easter and during the Pilgrimage Play season. When a fire damaged it in 1965, the county replaced it with a new cross of steel, plexiglass, and flourescent bulbs.

Less successful, at least during her lifetime, in bringing culture to Hollywood was oil heiress Aline Barnsdall. Aline Barnsdall purchased Olive Hill on June 3, 1919, for the purpose of establishing an art center. The property, consisting of thirty-six acres bounded by Hollywood Boulevard, Sunset Boulevard, Vermont Avenue and Edgemont Street, had been given its name in the 1890s by J.H. Spires, who planted the area extensively with olive trees. She intended to build a home for herself and an arts center, including a theater, art gallery, and library. Frank Lloyd Wright designed her home, which she called Hollyhock House after her favorite flower, patterning it after the mesa silhouette of the Pueblo Indians. With the help of Wright, Aline Barnsdall planted pine groves on the hill behind the house and great masses of eucalyptus to enclose them.

In 1923, Miss Barnsdall offered ten acres of the land to the city of Los Angeles as a gift, but the city did not accept the conditions she put on it. They did accept the property four years later, when Miss Barnsdall repeated her offer through the California Art Club. In 1931, she offered another eighteen acres to the city and was again turned down, at which point she erected large billboards on the property demanding that the city lease it, which it never did. Later, she used the billboards to express her views on a number of other subjects.

Just before Miss Barnsdall's death in 1946, Dorothy Clune Murray began converting the now-rundown property to an arts center, but years later

146

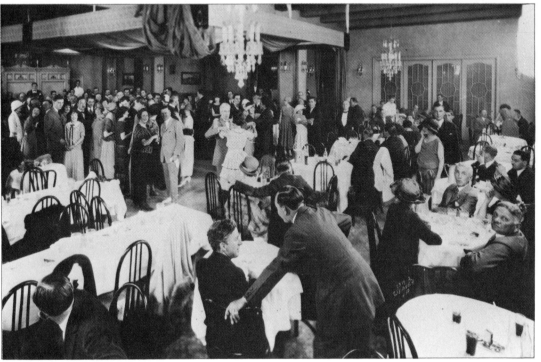

the site once again fell into disrepair. This was soon to be remedied when, in 1974, the city council approved Mayor Thomas Bradley's request to provide $500,000 to completely refurbish the magnificent house. The work was completed in July 1975. More than half a century after Aline Barnsdall envisioned it, Los Angeles finally had a permanent art center—Barnsdall Park.

Legitimate Theaters

Legitimate theaters in Hollywood grew side by side with the movie houses. In 1926, C.E. Toberman opened a tremendous theater, with a 120-foot-wide stage, called the El Capitan, across the street from the future site of Grauman's Chinese. The El Capitan's first presentation was a revue featuring British stars Beatrice Lillie, Jack Buchanan, and Gertrude Lawrence. It continued as a

Opposite page [1930]: The First Methodist Church at Franklin and Highland avenues. Top: The new fire station at Cahuenga and De Longpre avenues [1930]. Bottom: The northeast corner of Sunset and Vine, with its 1930 "almost new" automobile lot.

live theater until 1942, when it was adapted for movies and later renamed the Paramount Theater.

At about the same time, Frank Strong, Walter Wheat, and Elwood Riggs, who had leased Jacob Stern's new Plaza Hotel, built the Vine Street Theatre south of Hollywood Boulevard. When radio reached its heyday in Hollywood in the mid-1930s, the theater became a studio called the CBS Playhouse Theater, from which many of the network's shows were broadcast. In 1954, it reverted to the legitimate stage and was renamed the Huntington Hartford Theater.

The Vine Street Theatre was such a success that its three partners, together with S.H. Woodruff, opened the Hollywood Playhouse Theatre on Vine just north of Hollywood Boulevard in 1927.

Above: Another 1920s hot spot was the Hollywood Roof Ball Room, on the southwest corner of Vine and Selma; photo, 1930. Left: The YMCA, on the southwest corner of Selma and Hudson avenues, 1932. Opposite page: The Hollywood Playhouse, at 1735 Vine Street, 1930; the legitimate house later became the El Capitan, then the Hollywood Palace, and is today known simply as Palace, an entertainment complex.

The large, 1,148-seat theater became the home for *Ken Murray's Blackouts* in the 1940s and later proved to be ideal for television broadcasting. Renamed the Hollywood Palace, it hosted many television shows.

Restaurants

The boom in popular entertainment necessitated the opening of new and luxurious restaurants on Hollywood Boulevard. Musso & Frank Grill was an instant hit when it opened at 6669 Hollywood Boulevard in 1919. Founded by John Musso and Frank Toulet, they operated the small restaurant for six years, until they sold it to Joseph Carissimi and John Mosso, whose name was so similar to Musso.

For a while, Musso's [as it has always been called], was just about the only fine restaurant "on the boulevard." The movie people came, and still do, but without the glamour deemed necessary in other restaurants. It also became extremely popular with the local businessmen and merchants. In need of more room, the restaurant expanded in 1936 to 6667 Hollywood Boulevard, where it continued to increase in popularity, due to its extensive menu, well-prepared food, and fine service. Today it is the oldest restaurant in Hollywood and is owned and operated by Rose Keegel [John Mosso's daughter], Edith Carissimi [Joseph Carissimi's daughter-in-law], and Jesse Chavez. To many of those who have dined at Musso's, it is considered the finest

Above: A view of the Sunset Strip when it was a fairly desolate stretch of road, between Palm and La Cienega, 1932; the thoroughfare in the foreground is Holloway Drive.
Left: The Griffith Park Observatory under construction, 1933.
Right: Actress Claudette Colbert poses with her Christmas wreath on Vine, 1932.

Santa Claus

restaurant in Hollywood.

In 1923, Eddie Brandstatter opened the Montmartre Cafe down the street from the Hollywood Hotel. It was a movie-colony favorite during its brief history, and fans lined its sidewalk, stairways, and even foyer to catch sight of the stars. By 1929, the mobs of spectators were so dense that patrons began to complain. Brandstatter cut a passageway into the adjoining building and opened the private, and very exclusive, Embassy Club. However, without the adoring fans to reflect the patrons' egos, the stars quickly lost interest in both establishments.

One of Hollywood's finest and most popular restaurants, the Brown Derby, was opened on Valentine's Day, 1929, at 1628 North Vine Street in a building erected by Cecil B. DeMille. Founded by Herbert K. Somborn, he hired Robert H. Cobb

as combination steward, buyer, cashier, and occasional cook. After Somborn's death in 1934, Cobb was made president; shortly thereafter, he became the owner. With a collection of caricatures of movie stars hanging on the walls, and excellent cuisine, the Derby became immensely popular with both the motion picture personalities and the general public. At lunchtime, stars in costume and makeup would rush in from the sets to entertain friends or be interviewed by writers. Young movie hopefuls would eat frugally on money scrimped for the special occasion, all the while eating slowly and keeping a watchful eye for agents or friends who have made it in showbusiness and who might offer monetary or moral support, or for a studio

Above: Looking east
down Hollywood
Boulevard from Orange
Drive; the Hollywood
Hotel is at center—fronted
by palm trees. Right:
The Hollywood Athletic
Club, at Sunset and
Hudson [1933]; it has
been recently restored,
and operates as an
entertainment complex.

Above: Motion picture fans gather at
the main entrance to the Brown
Derby Restaurant on Vine for a glimpse
at the stars, 1933. Right: Young
movie hopefuls pose in front
of the new Hollywood Studio Club
on Lodi Place; photo taken in 1934.
Opposite page: Bing Crosby does
a scene with Shirley Chambers
in *Too Much Harmony*; director Edward
Sutherland [arm on script] looks
on. This was Bing's third picture
for Paramount, and by year's end
[1933], he would be listed
among the top ten box-office stars.

Above: Opening day at Farmers
Market, Fairfax and Third,
1934. Right: The fashionable
Innes Shoe Store on
Hollywood Boulevard, 1935.

Columbia Pictures, on Gower, between Sunset and Fountain, is one of the few studios that made it big on Poverty Row; 1935.

executive looking for "just the type." The Brown Derby can take credit—or the blame—for the introduction of telephones at tables during mealtimes. A loudspeaker system for paging and phone lines to each table were installed so that busy executives would not have to interrupt a luncheon. The number of times an agent or ad man was paged came to indicate the degree of popularity, and from time to time, these calls had been tabulated and the results circulated as the "Derby Derby."

Other restaurants patronized by picture personalities included the Hollywood Roof Ballroom at 1549 Vine Street, the Pig 'n Whistle at 6714 Hollywood; Henry's Delicatessen near Hollywood and La Brea; and the Armstrong-Carlton at 6600 Hollywood. Hollywood also boasted a highly respectable number of speakeasies during the days of Prohibition, some of which featured gambling as well as liquor. The Hollywood Division police gave the enforcement of the Volstead Act the same lack of priority it received in other large, cosmopolitan towns, much to the relief of Hollywood's celebrants. [Errol Flynn was famous for his gin recipe, which he supposedly prepared in the back room of the Hollywood Roosevelt Hotel's barber shop.]

The Crash

Hollywood was having a wonderful time and doing terrific business when the stock market crashed in October 1929. A place like Hollywood, where huge sums of capital were on the line in projects such as subdivisions, new stores, and studio expansion, was hit especially hard by the collapse of the big-money superstructure. Banks failed; the president of the Guaranty Building and Loan Association confessed to the embezzlement of $8 mil-

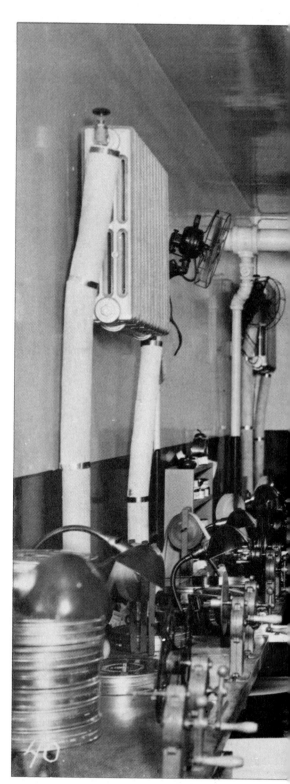

Top: Gower Gulch cowboys, on Sunset near Gower, await cast-
ing calls for extras in western films, 1936. Bottom: Hollywood
Boulevard at Las Palmas, looking east, 1935. Opposite page:
Film editors and splicers in an editing room, Columbia, 1935.

lion of the bank's assets. Hundreds of Hollywood depositors, large and small, were wiped out. Foreclosures were common, and many people lost homes and businesses.

At the time of the crash, the motion picture industry was still reeling from the advent of sound. Large studios, led by Warner Brothers, rushed to develop sound stages, recording equipment, and other technology for the new age of filmmaking. New technicians, musicians, and manual laborers had to be hired. All of this required an enormous capital outlay.

The conversion to sound also took an emotional toll on the industry. Many silent screen stars had come to Hollywood from abroad; it never occurred to anyone that their English was heavily accented until talkies came in. Others, even less fortunate, were discovered to have speaking voices completely inappropriate for the roles they had played in silent films. [John Gilbert, a romantic hero to millions, was the most notable casualty on this score—his high, wobbly voice made him ludicrous as a leading man.] Stage actors flocked to Hollywood as a result, and vocal coaches, who seemed to come out of the woodwork by the dozens, were the most lionized citizens in Hollywood.

Not only diction coaches thrived during the first depression years in Hollywood. Max Factor, a Russian immigrant who pioneered screen makeup, was supplying women throughout the world with the latest in beauty products by 1930. In 1935, he opened the Max Factor Hollywood Makeup Studio, which included a laboratory, research department, and manufacturing plant, in a gemlike building on Highland Avenue. The makeup studio soon became the meeting place for many of Hollywood's loveliest stars—including Lana Turner, Rita Hayworth, and Mona Freeman.

During the Thirties, the movies were shaken by the world's financial woes, but hardly toppled. They were too ingrained into America's entertainment habits to be deserted; in the darkest days of the depression, they brought too much sunshine to be ignored.

Top: Putting the finishing touches to the grounds of the new Griffith Park Observatory, a Hollywood landmark, 1935. Above: The six-year-old Hollywood Police Station on Wilcox, 1936.

At left: The Hollyhock House in Barnsdall Park was designed by Frank Lloyd Wright for its owner, Aline Barnsdall, who donated the house and ten acres to the city of Los Angeles in 1923. Wright's eldest son, Lloyd, supervised the building of it, and said that his father designed it to reflect a mesa silhouette, as originated by the Pueblo Indians. This photo was taken in 1935.

Opposite page, top: The boxing arena at the famed Hollywood Legion Stadium. Bottom left: The Hollywood Citizen News building on Wilcox. Above: Looking west down Hollywood Boulevard, at Vine Street. Right: Looking east on Hollywood Boulevard from Highland Avenue; the sign on the Montmartre Cafe is partially visible on left; all photos taken in 1936.

Top: Show host, Cecil B. DeMille
[facing away from camera],
talks to Gloria Swanson as
George Raft and June Lang look
on during a broadcast of
the popular *Lux Radio Theater*
from CBS Radio Playhouse, 1936.
At left: The CBS Radio Playhouse
was located in the Studio
Theatre [formerly the Vine
Street Theatre, which is
today the Huntington Hartford].

Above: Looking east on Hollywood Boulevard toward Cahuenga, 1937. At left: Hardly a day passes when someone isn't shooting film on the streets of Hollywood; in this 1936 photo, a camera has been set up in the middle of Hollywood Boulevard and is shooting a scene of pedestrians crossing the street, while a policeman detours traffic at the intersection of Hollywood & Vine.

Radio

The only rival movies had in the way of mass entertainment was radio which, by the 1930s, had come a long way from its crystal set beginnings. Hollywood acquired its first three radio stations in 1922; KNX, KHJ, and KFI, all marked by unreliable equipment and uncertain programming.

KNX began mainly as a promotion for the *Los Angeles Express*, when promotion manager Guy C. Earl gave away 1,000 crystal sets in a circulation campaign. In two years, KNX was broadcasting on a regular schedule from a Studebaker Sales Building at 6116 Hollywood Boulevard. Earl brought the hustler's promotion expertise to KNX. He provoked feuds with other radio stations and newspapers to gain publicity, sold advertising space to whoever wanted it, no matter how questionable the product, and broadcasted a murder trial, although his reporters were repeatedly thrown out of the courtroom. In 1928, Earl became a sportscasting pioneer. He broadcasted the Rose Bowl

Top: The original Don the Beachcomber Restaurant, on the east side of McCadden Place, north of Hollywood Boulevard; later, the restaurant relocated across the street. Bottom: The Sears Roebuck and Company celebration of its Santa Monica Blvd. store's third anniversary; both photos above were taken in 1936.

game via telephone—and sold the program to KFI.

KHJ was founded by Harry Chandler, publisher of the *Los Angeles Times.* It specialized in public affairs and children's programming. Its station identification theme was provided by singing canaries. Chandler sold the station to automobile dealer Don Lee in 1927. It became the CBS affiliate until 1936, when it joined the Mutual Network.

Packard dealer Earl C. Anthony founded KFI as an auto-promotion gimmick. He pioneered music and educational programming in an attempt to appeal to the upper middle-class audience that was Packard's main market. KFI was the first Western station to broadcast a live symphony orchestra [in 1924] and a live complete opera production; it produced the first broadcast from the Hollywood Bowl. It joined KPO in San Francisco in 1924 to form the first West Coast radio network. KFI became part of NBC's Red Network in 1927.

Columbia Broadcasting System built a $2 million facility—Columbia Square—at the corner of Sunset and Gower in 1938, making KNX its West Coast flagship station. NBC built a similar studio at Sunset and Vine the same year. Both facilities

Top: Clara Bow's "It" Cafe was located on the ground floor of the Hollywood Plaza building on Vine Street; the sign above the door and on the side of the building bears Clara's name and that of her husband, Rex Bell; photo, 1937. Bottom: The Colonial Drive-in Restaurant on Sunset Boulevard; photo, 1936.

boasted tremendous broadcast studios that accommodated large orchestras, state-of-the-art control rooms, and audiences of 300 or more.

In 1938, *Daily Variety* reported an expenditure of more than $18 million by six radio stations on programming, including $5 million on salaries for

600 film players. Although Hollywood still lagged behind New York as a national broadcast center, many network programs originated from here, employing 500 local writers and lyricists.

The film industry, in fact, found radio as strong a promotional tool as did newspapers and car dealers. Their players, broadcasting coast-to-coast, helped publicize new movies. Warner Brothers founded station KFWB in 1925, giving it space in its old administration building at Sunset and Bronson. Hearst columnist Louella Parsons took to radio like an executive to an expense account, and her signatory line—"This is Louella Parsons broadcasting from the Hollywood Hotel"—was heard throughout the nation.

Religious programming also had its birth in Hollywood when evangelist William Hogg arrived from Tennessee and was given a daily half-hour slot on KFAC in 1933. Hogg played a country

At right: The Garden of Allah, at 8150 Sunset Boulevard, has probably had more written about it than any other hostelry in the world, but then its habitues were among the most quotable and newsworthy literary and filmdom celebrities; they were a fast-living, hard-drinking, high-rolling lot who burned out fast and took the Garden with them; although its life as a hotel spanned only thirty-two years, the Garden of Allah had died of old age long before it was razed in 1959; photo 1937. Below: The Cafe Trocadero on the Sunset Strip; photo 1938.

At left: The famous Coconut Grove at the Ambassador Hotel on Wilshire Boulevard was only minutes away from Hollywood and was another playground of the stars. It was one of the first rooms on the West Coast to broadcast its orchestra and other entertainment on radio, when most listeners had only crystal sets to pull in the radio waves; photo, 1938.

Above: The number of behind-the-scenes people required to shoot one short scene for a film is always astonishing to tourists, but an economic boon to the film community. By 1920, when the Hollywood movie industry was less than ten years old, studio payrolls had already reached $25 million a year; the city's economy is very dependent upon the health of the movie industry. This scene is with Leah Ray and Anthony [Tony] Martin in *Sing and Be Happy*; photo, 1937. At right: The shops, buildings, and stages of the Columbia lot [now the Sunset-Gower Studios]; photo, 1938.

The Crossroads of the World shopping mall on Sunset Blvd. was declared an historical-cultural monument in 1974. It was opened October 29, 1936, and features a variety of old-world architecture, including Italian, French, Spanish, and Turkish. Next door is the Church of the Blessed Sacrament; photo, 1937.

preacher, Parson Josiah Hopkins, who rode the circuit of his rural parishioners in "Goose Creek." Hogg's wife, Virginia, played a character named "Sister Sarah." The show was entitled "The Country Church of Hollywood," and by 1932 was heard coast-to-coast daily over the CBS network. Reverend Hogg built an actual nondenominational Country Church of Hollywood in a grove of trees on Argyle near Hollywood Boulevard. When he died in 1937, "Sister Sarah" continued the broadcasts until her death in 1965. Today, the church, with its congregation of three hundred members, is under the capable leadership of Josiah's and Sarah's daughter, Martha Hogg.

The Greek Theatre and Other Projects

Civic projects continued despite the hard times. The City Board of Park Commissioners de-

cided that 1930 was a good year to make use of the trust fund Colonel Griffith J. Griffith had willed to the city [along with Griffith Park] when he died in 1919. He had called for a Greek Theater, an observatory, and a hall of science to be built on Mt. Hollywood.

The Greek Theatre, with outdoor seating for 4500, was completed in September 1930. An indication of the depressed prices of the times was the $150 nightly rental, plus five percent of the gate, charged a grand opera company in 1931.

Colonel Griffith's instructions were so specific that the city had to break his will to locate the Griffith Observatory farther down the mountain. Griffith had neglected to consider the growing dominance of the automobile, and his directions

for construction of the observatory and hall of science called for the use of a streetcar and funicular railway to get to it. Work began in 1933 and was completed in 1935, at a site that included parking space for cars.

One of Hollywood's most dramatic tragedies occurred during the observatory construction, when four thousand welfare workers were confronted with a fire that had broken out at the mouth of Dam Canyon on the east side of Mt. Hollywood. Many workers streamed down the canyon to fight the brush fire; the wind changed suddenly and carried the thick smoke into their midst. Twenty-seven were found dead after the fire was contained.

The Hollywood Hospital was in deep financial trouble during the depression and was bailed out by a half-million dollar trust fund left by Mrs. Millicent Olmsted, who had left her money for the establishment of a Christian hospital. The Olmsted Memorial trustees took control of the Hollywood Hospital in 1937, changing its name to Hollywood Presbyterian Hospital—Olmsted Memorial. Today it is known simply as Hollywood Presbyterian Medical Center.

In 1934, Roger Dahlhjelm got the idea that would create one of the most successful and longest-lasting attractions in the Hollywood area. He envisioned an empty field in which farmers could sell their produce directly to the public, eliminating the middlemen and charging lower prices.

Top: The huge NBC Radio City complex dominated the northeast block of Sunset and Vine from 1938 to 1964, on the former site of the Jesse Lasky Feature Play Company; the complex housed eight studios, four of them with a seating capacity for 350 persons. Right: The enormous wall mural that overpowered the lobby of the NBC Radio City complex was symbolic of radio's vast power and influence in the third and fourth decades of the century; indeed, it was radio that made the two-block stretch of Vine between Hollywood and Sunset boulevards the hub of entertainment activity in Hollywood and made the intersection of Hollywood and Vine famous. Bottom: The original El Capitan Theatre was one of the city's first legitimate theaters; it became a movie house and was renamed the Paramount in 1942. All photos taken in 1938.

Left, top: CBS Radio, on Sunset near Gower, is just two blocks east of the NBC Radio City site, and looks much today as it did when these 1938 photos were taken. Left: A crowd forms in the CBS forecourt, waiting to see a CBS radio show. Above: A live radio broadcast. Right: The sound-effects personnel work a live radio broadcast; the backbone of radio drama and comedy, the sound-effects departments often created ingenius aural illusions.

Above left: A live dramatic broadcast with a full orchestral accompaniment, CBS Radio, 1938. Top right: By 1938, the CBS Radio Playhouse had taken over the old Vine Street Theatre; two years earlier, the building was called the Studio Theatre, but now the old marquee has been removed and CBS is the sole tenant, owing largely to the huge success of such radio shows as the *Lux Radio Theater*, which brought movie stars to radio.

Earl Gilmore told Dahlhjelm that he could use part of his father's old farm at the corner of Third and Fairfax. Dahlhjelm recruited some farmers and opened the concession in July 1934.

It was a collection of eighteen canvas-covered booths called, appropriately enough, Farmers Market. Twelve of the farmers sold fruits and vegetables, while the others sold such items as wine and homemade cakes. It captured the imagination of local residents and of tourists from around the country, immediately becoming a community landmark from its opening. Today it houses more than 160 stalls and shops and is one of the area's most popular tourist attractions.

Another pioneer shopping center was the Crossroads of the World, which opened October 29, 1936. Located on the northern side of Sunset Boulevard, just east of Las Palmas Avenue, the unique complex was designed by architect Robert V. Derrah for owner, Ella Crawford. In order to develop the property to the fullest, and provide a maximum of store frontage, a private street scheme or mall was developed with access at Sunset, Selma, and Las Palmas Avenues. To this, the exclusion of automobile traffic and the numerous fine old trees lent an old-world atmosphere in contrast to the busy streets of Hollywood. On one side of the mall were buildings of Italian and French architecture, and on the other, Spanish and Mexican, while in the center was a marine-modern structure surmounted by a 60-foot tower on which a world

eight feet in diameter revolved. Farther up the mall were buildings of Moorish and Turkish design, while the entrance from Las Palmas Avenue was a narrow crooked street reminiscent of old Cape Cod. In December of 1974, thirty-eight years after its dedication, the Crossroads of the World was declared a historical-cultural monument by the Los Angeles Cultural Heritage Board.

The same year that Farmers Market opened, oil tycoon Earl Gilmore built Gilmore Stadium. Located near the intersection of Fairfax Avenue and Beverly Boulevard, it was structured with a seating capacity of 18,000. It was known as the working man's stadium because popular prices prevailed during the latter days of the depression. It was at Gilmore Stadium that professional football in Los Angeles was played and eventually became a paying commercial venture. Midget-automobile racing was developing into a national sport, and the stadium became the training ground for the top drivers of Indianapolis-type racing cars. Every conceivable form of outdoor entertainment was promoted successfully at Gilmore Stadium. A few years later, Earl Gilmore built Gilmore Field, which became the home for the Hollywood Stars baseball team.

Part Three:
1939-1959

On Sunday morning, December 7, 1941, Hollywood stirred late to a sparkling day. It was a good day to enjoy the great Southern California outdoors. Some would take in one of the all-time great films playing in downtown Hollywood: *The Great Dictator, Citizen Kane,* and *Sergeant York.* Evangelist Aimee Semple McPherson advertised two sermons for the day: "One Foot in Heaven," and "Keep 'em Flying," both titles of current films.

Hollywood talk buzzed about the antiaircraft artillery soldiers who had taken over Hollywood Park, anticipating enemy salvos. More frivolous chatter broke the mounting tension. Residents, celebrities, and hometown folks alike talked of Harry Warner's new granddaughter, of last night's auction of blooded cattle, of the hot bidding in Hollywood over cowboy "property" Gene Autry, of the dazzling Hollywood couple, Clark Gable and Carole Lombard.

Suddenly, radio bulletins jolted the community. Pearl Harbor was under attack by the Japanese. The stunning news set Hollywood back. Dazed, the community strained with the reality, as did all Americans. Downtown, civilians and servicemen on leave gathered solemnly on street corners. Los Angeles' Little Tokyo transformed into a ghost town. The next day, Japanese employees of movie studios were told not to report for work until the government had ruled on their status. They never returned; they were carted away to "relocation camps," as the outdoor prisons were euphemistically called.

One studio hastily shelved a planned musical called *Pearl Harbor Pearl.* Another dropped the title, *I'll Take Manila.*

The day after the United States was forced into the Second World War, Hollywood became a military camp. Within a day, 100 studio trucks and drivers were transporting army troops and equipment, studio arsenals were stripped of prop rifles, machine guns, revolvers, and ammunition to fortify undersupplied posts along the West Coast.

Movie studios mobilized their fire-fighting equipment for the war effort. The beautiful beaches in front of Hollywood's luxurious homes at Malibu soon swarmed with soldiers abruptly moved from inland training camps. The West Coast was preparing for a potential Japanese attack.

Although the Japanese never did attack the mainland—other than the twenty-five shells pumped into an oilfield at Ellswood, twelve miles north of Santa Barbara, by a Japanese submarine—there was one terrifying "counterattack" by nervous American antiaircraft gunners, launched on February 25, 1942, less than three months after the attack on Pearl Harbor.

Above: Awaiting the arrival of celebrities, hundreds of movie fans gather at the Pantages during a premiere in 1939; the Pantages opened on June 4, 1930, played host to the Academy Awards presentations for ten years, and showed its last film in January 1977; the following month, it joined the nearby Aquarius and Huntington Hartford as a legitimate theater.

Big artillery guns hidden in the coastline hills flashed into action against unidentified aircraft flying overhead. Observers in the heart of Hollywood could plainly see searchlights poke long silver probes into the sky, while antiaircraft batteries spat 1,430 rounds of searing ack-ack—at what, no one knew. Golden yellow tracer bullets and high-explosive shells raced toward the stars, much like massive Fourth of July fireworks familiar to Hollywood. Unfamiliar to Hollywood, however, these fireworks returned to earth like metal hail on slumbering rooftops. No "enemy" planes were hit, but at least two civilians were killed in car accidents caused by the blackout. A few houses were badly damaged and many windows smashed. People were petrified. Americans had never experienced guns of war on their soil, nor were they sophisticated about blackouts.

"I watched a bunch of people form into a mob when the blackout wasn't immediately effective everywhere," said Vernon Farquhar, a long-time Hollywood resident and former president of the Hollywood Chamber of Commerce. "They went berserk, smashing lights everywhere. They threw rocks at the big Pep Boys sign. Then they broke into businesses to dash lights. The blackout took time to spread uniformly and these folks weren't waiting."

In Washington D.C. the next day, the secretary of the navy declared the alleged attack a false alarm. Secretary of War Henry Stimson reported that some fifteen unidentified aircraft had flown over Hollywood and Los Angeles, but he believed they were private planes operated by enemy agents bent on spying. Speculation on the cause of

Movie extras and fans outside the famous Marathon-Street entrance to Paramount Pictures, 1939.

their overflight continued for months but no one was ever certain what had actually occurred.

Hollywood was never again harassed by the phantom aircraft or the lone Japanese submarine, but a steady stream of alleged and strange sightings of the sky continued throughout the war years, and even a year afterward.

Hollywood, however, did not need the incentive of false—or real—attacks to get behind the war effort in a big way. The small town had been growing into a war town before the attack on Pearl Harbor, even more so than other American cities. Nearby army and navy camps swelled in size, defense plants expanded, studio buildings were camouflaged, blackout regulations were enforced, and air-raid shelters, complete with hospital units, were built on studio lots.

And Hollywood had its city service problems: shortages of housing, food, transportation. But Hollywood had its film colony, unlike the rest of the country, and it immersed itself into the survival struggle. Hundreds of entertainers joined war organizations, such as the Red Cross, the USO, Naval Aid Auxiliary, canteen services, the American Women's Voluntary Services, and the Army Camps Emergency Services. Many stars joined the military to fight: Clark Gable, Jimmy Stewart, Robert Taylor, Gene Raymond, Robert Montgomery, and Victor Mature, to name but a few. Others made training films for the services.

Hollywood, naturally, made many feature films with heavily anti-Fascist themes. And more escape films were made to lighten the hearts of war-weary Americans. Musicals and comedies were big fare. This was the era of Abbott and Costello and the leggy aqua-star Esther Williams.

Statistics of the times indicate that some seventy percent of Hollywood's community families had members in the armed services, some 29,000 in all. This somber and patriotic figure flies

In New York, *Earl Carroll's Vanities* ran from 1923 to 1936, but the police were constantly raiding the show, and Carroll's fortune was being depleted, so he built the Earl Carroll Theatre in Hollywood and opened it December 26, 1938. The revue was an enormous success, and ran until Carroll died in an airplane accident on June 17, 1948. Today it is the Aquarius Theatre.

Below: The 1939 Hollywood Stars baseball club played its games at Gilmore Stadium—corner of Fairfax and Beverly Boulevard. The team was owned by a group of celebrities, including George Burns, Gracie Allen, Gary Cooper, Walt Disney & Bing Crosby.

Above: The lounge of the Earl Carroll Theatre looks much the same today as it did when this photo was taken [c.1940]. Opposite page: The Hollywood Hotel's rules and regulations were printed on fabric banners and posted in each suite; photo, c.1940.

Hollywood : Hotel :

RULES AND REGULATIONS

Guests are requested to lock their doors on RETIRING and also to lock them when going out.

Do not drive tacks or nails in the walls or wood work.

Money, jewelry and all valuables must be deposited in the safe in the office, otherwise the proprietor will not be responsible for any loss.

Persons engaging rooms will be charged for them from the time they are placed at their disposal, whether occupied or not.

Washing will be promptly attended to by leaving orders at the office.

Children will not be allowed to make a play-ground of the parlors or hallways.

Please turn out lights on retiring or leaving the room.

The proprietor will not be responsible for loss or damage to wearing apparel.

Vocal or instrumental music will not be permitted before 10 a. m. or after 9:30 p. m.

No trunks or baggage will be allowed to remain in the halls.

Rubbish must not be thrown in slop jars or carried to the water closets.

All damage to the furniture will be charged to the occupant of the room.

Guests without baggage are requested to PAY IN ADVANCE.

All accounts must be settled on rendering statement.

The manager will not be responsible for washing given outside the house.

Guests desiring to be called at an early hour will please notify the clerk.

Guests who intend to depart on an early morning train will find it a great convenience to settle their bills on the evening previous.

Guests vacating rooms must notify office before 1 P. M. otherwise usual charge will be made.

The management reserves the right to enter and inspect rooms and furniture at any time.

Baggage, furniture or pictures stored for guests will be at owner's risk.

Dogs, cats, or parrots will not be permitted in the rooms.

Disorderly conduct on the part of the guests will secure their immediate dismissal from the house.

No washing or ironing will be permitted in rooms or bathrooms.

The Law to Regulate the Liability of Hotel Keepers.

Civil Code, California.

Baggage will be held for unpaid bills according to law.—Sec. 1863 Civil Code of California.

GEO. L. KROM, Mgr.

The RKO Studios at Melrose & Gower. In 1948, millionaire Howard Hughes bought controlling interest in RKO and later assumed management of all production at the studio. In the 60s, the facility was bought by Desilu; today it's part of Paramount Pictures. Left: The Florentine Gardens on Hollywood Blvd. Both photos were taken in 1940.

The Santa Claus Lane Parade, 1940. This Hollywood tradition began in 1928, with Santa riding down the boulevard for all the children to see. But no floats joined the parade until 1932.

in the face of the image many Americans have of Hollywood as a community of irresponsible, ego-centric children.

Hollywood, in fact, had much more in common with other American communities than its glamour image led many to believe. Long before Pearl Harbor, there were many in Hollywood's film industry who sensed the growing menace of Fascism in Europe and elsewhere. Such an understanding was later dubbed by some in the United States as "premature anti-Fascism." Political study groups were formed in Hollywood, and entertainers began the fight against Facism, especially by supporting Spanish Republicans against Franco and Hitler. This anti-Fascist sentiment grew faster and sooner in Hollywood than elsewhere, because many of the motion picture industry's artists and technicians came from all nations and races, and before Pearl Harbor, its pictures were produced for a world market. That market shrank as Fascist-minded market countries banned American films.

In the three years before the U.S. entered the war, the film industry produced more than one thousand feature pictures; fifty were anti-Nazi.

The bulk of filmfare was not political but, from a small and highly vocal group of people, the anti-Fascist films brought the baseless charge that Hollywood was inciting the American populace to war. As 1941 drew to a close, a Senate subcommittee began an investigation of Hollywood's alleged "war mongering." Wendell Willkie, defending the industry, soon had the accusers on the defensive, and the investigation withered on the eve of the attack on Pearl Harbor.

Scarcely a branch of film production remained unaffected by the war. Travel restrictions imposed by the government discouraged the use of distant film locations. Most filming occurred in or around Hollywood itself. No cameras were allowed near army reservations, dams, or war plants. Sea shots were forbidden in harbors from Seattle to San Diego. Train shots were impossible; the government had requisitioned all of the nation's available rolling stock. Air raid blackout regulations eliminated night filming.

189

Top: The widening of the Cahuenga Pass to accommodate increased traffic, 1940. Left: The north side of Hollywood Boulevard, looking west from McCadden, 1940. Right: A live broadcast of the Gene Autry show at CBS Columbia Square on Sunset. Gene, in white suit and hat, is at right; the other three in white hats [seated at left] are his Cass County Boys. Photo taken 1940.

These restrictions relaxed with the mounting months of war, but the industry had learned valuable lessons in economy. Before the war, Hollywood was profligate in spending. But with the war economy, it learned to become a miser as lavish sets were ruled out. There was a materials shortage to such an extent that in some studios even the production-set nails were hand counted and sorted by size.

Hollywood's artisans of make-believe outdid even their own miracle makings. Wood took the place of concrete and masonry. When a fire scene was shot, an asbestos screen was painted to look like wood. Hidden gas jets were ignited and the cameras caught a realistic shot of a burning house. But nothing was damaged. Sets were constructed that could be adapted to multiple uses. Their framework was permanent, but windows, doors, and fireplaces were removable. By ingenious alterations, a nightclub could be made to look like a hotel lobby, an airport terminal, or a railroad station. Studios swapped expensive movable sets—

Sunset Plaza Square, on the Sunset Strip; the building in the
center was then occupied by Bundles for Britain, Inc.; 1941.

Top: The Palladium, on Sunset Bouelvard, 1941. Above: Marie
Wilson was the perennial star of *Ken Murray's Blackouts*;
the show played for seven years, two months, and three
days, and Miss Wilson played 3,126 consecutive
performances. Right: Looking south across Sunset
Boulevard at the Garden of Allah, 1943; many of the
twenty-five tile-roofed bungalows are visible;
across Crescent Heights [on the left] from the parking
lot, is Schwab's Pharmacy [not shown], where Lana Turner
was not discovered—she was discovered in a soda
fountain across from Hollywood High; a savings and loan
now occupies the Garden site, but a parking lot remains,
along with a small park containing a model of the Garden.

replicas of ships, for example.

Counting nails by hand became too tedious and time consuming. An enterprising technician invented a device resembling a carpet sweeper that picked up stray nails; another device was invented that would then sort and even straighten them. Hardware fixtures were replaced with glass or plastic. Hairpins—studios were limited to two pounds a month—were checked in and out of dressing rooms as if they were priceless. They were used, sterilized, and used again. When Chinese imports were stopped, makeup workers discontinued making wigs of human hair. Camel's hair brushes used to apply makeup were sent to aircraft plants for use in dusting precision instruments. Extravagant car-pursuit scenes, wasting rubber tires and gasoline, became past memories.

Hollywood had drastically limited its raw film consumption, and directors were instructed to rehearse scenes thoroughly before turning on the cameras. Actors were advised to come on the set

Above: Charlie Morrison's Mocambo was open from 1939 to 1958. Right: Dr. Jules Stein [in suit, and of MCA fame] and contractor Al Ybarra accompany Bette Davis and John Garfield at the Hollywood Canteen construction site. Both photos, 1942.

with lines well memorized.

Tightening belts forced the secession of Hollywood's famed Santa Claus Parade. When the war was over, the parade resumed on November 23, 1945, to a record crowd of cheering onlookers.

As the war lengthened, more defense workers and servicemen poured into an already overburdened town. Housing became a serious problem. By the end of 1944, it seemed as if every service person in Southern California with a forty-eight hour pass descended on the film capital.

Nevertheless, Hollywood provided America's fighting men and women a warm and often glamorous welcome. Studios that had closed their doors to tourists, opened them to servicemen with overseas records, who often went on special tours of the lots and were invited to meet their favorite

stars.

Where war films were produced, military personnel were allowed to watch the make-believe scenes they had lived through on the battlefield. Sometimes a soldier met an actor costumed in the uniform of a general. So real was the "officer" to the soldier that he would snap to attention and salute.

On weekends, soldiers outnumbered civilians ten to one on the streets of downtown Hollywood. At first, they had to sleep in parks or in the aisles and lobbies of theaters. But once aware of the uncomfortable overcrowding, Hollywood unfurled its hospitality. Dormitories and auditoriums in schools and churches were made available to them, and private home owners offered bedrooms. California's theater owners collected $190,000 from audiences in a "Beds for Buddies" campaign to match what the state of California contributed.

The closest thing to home for fighters on a Hollywood furlough was "Mom" Lehr's Hollywood Guild and Canteen, at 1284 North Crescent Heights Boulevard. To thousands from all the allied nations who sought temporary refuge in Hollywood, "Mom's" place was the nearest berth to heaven. On an average, 800 stayed there each week night, with as many as 1,200 on weekends.

Lehr's canteen offered clean, comfortable beds, three square meals a day, and the privilege of coming and going as one pleased. There was no time limit either. And if hunger struck at early hours of the morning, the icebox and kitchen facilities were always available.

Anne Lehr was in charge of a small charity organization when she decided to help servicemen. She had cared for Hollywood's broken-down stuntmen, the unemployed and underfed extras of the entertainment industry. But when Hawaii was at-

tacked, she shifted focus. Many of her guests took jobs in war plants, leaving her nearly alone in the former mansion of silent screen star Dustin Farnum.

The outgoing humanitarian noticed servicemen walking Hollywood streets at night, sleeping on benches, in doorways or in parked cars. Neither the USO nor any of the canteens that offered a good time were designed to serve as temporary hostelries for the often indigent soldiers. Lehr decided to turn her sanctuary into a free hotel for the fighters of fascism. She and a small group of helpers foraged for thirty-five beds, and on May 15, 1942, the Hollywood Guild and Canteen opened to an *empty* house.

"Mom" had been so preoccupied arranging a home for her future adoptees that she had neglected to publicize her offer. Several of her assistants, in despair at the emptiness of the guild, drove down Hollywood Boulevard collecting servicemen.

Opposite page: Actress Paulette Goddard signs autographs for servicemen at the Hollywood Canteen, 1943. Above: Bringing smiles to the faces of servicemen was Danny Kaye's avocation during the war, and he often entertained at the Canteen; 1943.

Soldiers were skeptical. "What's the catch, lady," some asked. Several took a chance and cautiously consented to come along. About fifty ended up at the guild that first night and devoured a turkey dinner. After a sound night's sleep and a hearty breakfast, they left happy. The word spread, Lehr's aides continued to search the streets for a few nights, until servicemen began appearing at the hostel of their own volition. The guild quickly became known as "Mom's," and acquired a reputation everywhere in the world the soldiers traveled.

Besides the huge main house, new structures were built and nearby buildings were used. Soon, there were hundreds of beds, with more in an abandoned market a block away. A private house

in the next block was home to another 100 military men on leave.

The Hollywood Guild and Canteen was governed by a board consisting of Hollywood stars: Mary Pickford, Janet Gaynor, and Myrna Loy. But direction came from Anne Lehr. She arrived to work at 6 P.M. and stayed until early the next morning. Lehr eventually had 1,000 women helpers; they cleaned, washed dishes, made the beds, waited tables, and danced with the servicemen.

The men themselves had complete run of the place, and often helped care for it. They drank $100 worth of milk a day, and consumed more than 1,400 eggs at each breakfast. Visitors ate all they wanted at any time of day.

Such an operation was expensive and could not last without financial aid. One of Hollywood's

Top: Servicemen pose outside the Canteen, located on Cahuenga just south of Sunset; photo, 1944. Left: There was a waiting list for volunteer Canteen hostesses, who were very carefully chosen and supervised; here a few of them do the jitterbug with servicemen on leave in Hollywood; photo, 1943. Above: Incomparable Marlene Dietrich dances with a soldier. The two are surrounded by members of the army and army air corps waiting to cut in. Right: Mickey Rooney sits in with the orchestra; photo, 1943.

Above: The forty-foot cross, built as a memorial to Christine Stevenson, founder of the Pilgrimage Play, sits at the top of a hill overlooking the Cahuenga Pass. It was dedicated in 1923, and destroyed and rebuilt in 1965. Right: A war bond sales office at the entrance to the Hollywood Bowl; photo taken in 1942.

influential entertainment trade newspapers, *The Hollywood Reporter,* carried an editorial by its owner-publisher, W.R. Wilkerson, praising "Mom's" as the best effort Hollywood had contributed to the war. In it he appealed to the movie studios to save the guild. Hedda Hopper, Louella Parsons, and other established Hollywood celebrities echoed his plea. Nils Thor Granlund took nightly collections at the Florentine Gardens, amounting to about $1,000 weekly. Beryl Wallace did the same at Earl Carroll's nightclub. The Hollywood Canteen contributed $52,000 annually. The major studios added another $40,000, and the smaller ones contributed $50,000.

A corner of Hollywood and Vine, 1943; it has changed very little.

"Mom" Lehr didn't stop helping servicemen after the war. She worked with rehabilitation programs, and many ex-servicemen still called the Hollywood Guild and Canteen home while attending school under the GI Bill of Rights.

Today, a huge apartment complex for singles, the Tennis Club Apartments, stands where the guild once housed tens of thousands of soldiers. On the exact spot where the mansion once rocked with R & R gaiety, now sits a tennis court used by the tenants who live in the furnished apartments.

Vacationing soldiers had other places for entertainment in Hollywood, but the most glamorous and most frequented was the Hollywood Canteen on Cahuenga Boulevard, just south of Sunset Boulevard. A massive five-story parking complex now occupies the site.

Bette Davis and John Garfield founded the Hollywood Canteen along with the support of Dr. Jules Stein. Columbia Studios dedicated the opening of its film hit, *The Talk of the Town*, to the canteen. Held at the swanky Ciro's nightclub, the event turned into one of the biggest movie fund-raisers of the decade, netting the canteen $6,500.

Once a stable and then a little theater, the Hollywood Canteen rented for $100 a month. Task committees formed, materials were gathered, and hundreds of skilled volunteers remodeled and equipped the building. Three weeks later, the project represented a value of more than $15,000. One person put up $200; the rest was donated labor. The finished product looked like it might have been two red-planked New England barns thrown together, cleaned up, and redecorated. The walls sported western murals painted by film artists, cartoonists, and other artists of local and national reputation.

Gargantuan beams supported the ceiling. The chandeliers were wagon wheels with pendant kerosene lanterns converted to electricity. There were tables, chairs, a dance floor, a stage, and a snack bar running the length of the room.

The Hollywood Canteen opened October 3, 1942, with Eddie Cantor as master of ceremonies. The grand opening was tailored like a premiere at

An Easter Sunrise Service at the Hollywood Bowl; photo, 1944.

the Chinese Theatre. Four bands entertained: Rudy Vallee and his Coast Guard band, Kay Kyser's band, Duke Ellington, and a band from the Santa Ana Air Base. Bud Abbott and Lou Costello and many other entertainers were on hand.

Eventually, 6,000 stars, players, writers, directors, and secretaries were registered to work as hosts, bus persons, kitchen crews, and general helpers. It took 300 volunteers to operate the canteen in two shifts between 7:00 P.M. and midnight.

The uniform of any branch of service in the united allied forces sufficed for admission. Those in civilian clothes were helpers or entertainers, who were fingerprinted and registered to prevent illicit vice and prostitution. Fire regulations limited the capacity to 500 at a time; however, 2,000 men a night was the average attendance.

With no limit to consumption, everything inside was free: cigarettes, milk, coffee, sandwiches and cake. Two name bands performed nightly, coordinated by the Musicians' Mutual Protective Association, Locals 47 and 767. Conservatively estimated, the music provided was worth about $1 million a year. The soldiers deeply appreciated this entertainment.

Among the volunteers were many of the most attractive women stars, including Betty Grable, Olivia de Havilland, Joan Leslie, Carole Landis, Greer Garson, Deanna Durbin, and Anne Shirley. Although they dressed simply to lend informality to their roles as hostesses, their presence still overwhelmed the star-struck, youthful military men. Some 3,500 junior hostesses were registered, and a long waiting list was ever present. While they all danced with the service personnel, they were not

Top left: Entrance to Mom Lehr's Guild-Canteen. Right: Bunks set up for servicemen on leave. The Guild-Canteen [not to be confused with the Hollywood Canteen], provided 24-hour-a-day meals and nearly a thousand beds for servicemen who converged on Hollywood by the hundreds from nearby bases; photo, 1943.

allowed to reveal their phone numbers, addresses, or last names. Officially, they were forbidden to date the GIs.

The effervescent and ever-popular Marlene Dietrich worked at everything from cutting cake, washing dishes, and serving at the snack bar, to performing. Singer Walter Woolf King was the master of ceremonies, and arranged special programs for two super floor shows every night. Chef Guiseppe Milani supervised the food program. Through his cunning, he was able to have most of the food, refreshments and cigarettes donated.

The Hollywood Canteen was also open Sunday afternoon, and usually offered concerts with John Charles Thomas, Nelson Eddy, Jeanette MacDonald, and other top singers.

Eddie Cantor and George Jessel were regular attractions. Eddie would sometimes bring his radio show over from NBC, and Charlie McCarthy frequently brought in Edgar Bergen [or so Charlie claimed]. Kay Kyser, Red Skelton, Rudy Vallee, Dinah Shore, Betty Hutton, Ginny Simms and many more regularly performed.

Mothers of film stars took over the canteen's work every Monday, acting as hosts, kitchen crew, and snack bar servers. The soldiers enjoyed talking with the mothers of idolized stars.

No other entertainment establishment in the world had such an impressive array of bus boys as

did the canteen. Fred MacMurray, Basil Rathbone, John Loder, John Garfield, George Murphy, Louis Calhern, and Jean Gabin were among the male stars who bussed dishes and cleaned up.

With few exceptions, every major radio and screen entertainer in Hollywood volunteered at the canteen. Studio secretaries were on hand to take dictation and help the soldiers get messages ready for mail. An estimated 100,000 young men visited the canteen monthly. In one month, they consumed 4,000 loaves of bread, 400 pounds of butter, 1,500 pounds of coffee, 50,000 half pints of milk, 1,000 pounds of cheese, and all the sandwich meat they could get. In addition, there were 40,000 gallons of fruit punch, 75,000 packages of cigarettes, and 150,000 pieces of cake.

The Hollywood Canteen was mustered out on November 22, 1945, shortly after the war's end. The last night's festivities, with quips from Bob Hope, Jack Benny and Jerry Colonna, brought a sorrowful end to the canteen, which had been open every day for three years.

Hollywood, during the war, also had the distinction of having the longest-running variety revue in the history of American legitimate theater.

Ken Murray's Blackouts played continuously in Hollywood from June 24, 1942, to August 27, 1949. The show played 3,874 performances to millions of patrons, and grossed $7 million. Murray assembled a large team of talent to back up his star comedienne Marie Wilson. Over the years, he employed 1,456 people and helped launch the careers of 100 celebrities, such as Rhonda Fleming, Cara Williams, and Mary Ford.

Apart from putting energy into entertaining troops on R & R, Hollywood celebrities and industry workers of all kinds—some 240,000 members of the motion picture and allied entertainment fields—had sold bonds and solicited blood for the wounded.

Top box office stars like Bob Hope and Bing Crosby contributed greatly to war bond drives. Al Jolson and Eddie Cantor were also among the top war bond sellers. Others who sold bonds made additional war efforts. Marlene Dietrich, Betty Grable, Dorothy Lamour, Lana Turner, and other women stars boosted morale by posing for barrack pinups. In Albuquerque, Ginger Rogers sold her dancing shoes for $10,000 in bonds. Someone in the crowd asked to wear her hat, bought it for $50,000 in bonds, and returned it. Veronica Lake auctioned off a lock of her hair for $185,000 in bonds. In Portland, a young man used his savings to buy a $5,000 war bond from Lana Turner and, under the influence of a kiss from the actress, ran off to join the navy.

The war was brought home to Hollywood in a deep personal way when the airliner carrying Carole Lombard from an Indianapolis bond rally crashed and burned. The small town of Hollywood learned firsthand what it felt like to have a popular hometown person killed in the war effort. After the shock of her death settled, Lombard's husband, the famed Clark Gable, signed up to fight.

By 1944, when the U.S. Treasury initiated three bond-selling campaigns, motion picture exhibitors across the nation were credited with twenty percent of "E" bond sales. Movie theaters emphasized direct sales to patrons. During the year, more than 15,000 Bond Premieres were held,

The school and Church of the Blessed Sacrament; the school was opened in 1923; the church opened in June 1928; photo, 1944.

with distributors supplying pictures without charge and exhibitors giving up cash admissions for audiences composed exclusively of bond buyers. On December 7, 1944, theater owners commemorated Pearl Harbor by sponsoring a Free-Movie Day for bond purchasers. Proceeds topped all similar campaigns. Exhibitors urged patrons to "get in the scrap," and nearby parking lots filled up with stockpiles of copper collected mostly by youths. By the end of 1944, these theater-going salvage experts had rounded up 324 million pounds of rags, rubber, copper, and other vital materials.

Theater owners also made appeals for blood donations. Visual demonstrations on the screen prompted thousands to sign up at theater exits and make blood donations later. Before the war, most theater managers refused to solicit funds for any cause because it interrupted carefully timed programs and often annoyed audiences. But when the war jolted the people, exhibitors and audiences

The Vallera Italian Kitchen was a favorite spot, especially during radio's heyday; it was located on the northwest corner of Argyle and Hollywood Boulevard; today it's a bank. Photo taken 1944.

alike rallied to the cause. The result was that the motion picture industry helped enormously in the meeting of wartime needs; its power to inform and to influence 85 million moviegoers a week was most productive.

Hollywood's spirit in the 1940s was still that of a small, close-knit family town with the added morale booster of a war to draw people together. The division between Hollywood celebrities and the average citizens was nearly nonexistent in those times. People helped each other out. Vernon Farquhar, then owner of Hollywood Tire Company, recounts a story that illustrates this fraternity.

"In the war years, you couldn't buy tires, hardly. Only used ones were sometimes available, and retreads were not obtainable either. It was hard to make a living for a tire businessman then. A friend of mine walked into the store one day and asked how I was making it. I could claim to be doing poorly only. He asked if I could borrow from a bank. No bank would loan me money since my business wasn't going well. He then said, 'Well, Vernon, here's $5,000 to tide you over.' I was touched, but I couldn't accept, since I didn't know how I could pay it back. He said, 'I didn't say anything about paying it back.'

"You know, you can't hardly find anyone around like that anymore."

When President Truman announced, on August 14, 1945, that the war with Japan was over, Hollywood—like the rest of the nation—went wild. The streets snowed with confetti. Servicemen and civilians danced in the streets; an impromptu parade paralyzed traffic for hours. Red Cars were jerked from their wires; power stopped, as did traffic. Through the night, 3,000 servicemen jammed the Hollywood Canteen.

The hot war was over. The cold war came quickly on its heels.

The Cold War Splits Hollywood

Motion picture-making is a major Hollywood industry. What happens to it affects the broader community of Hollywood, sometimes profoundly, sometimes tangentially only. The industry's high profile often attracts applause and attacks that affect the entire nation. The years immediately following World War II were dramatic transitional

When victory over Japan was announced, nearly everyone in Hollywood took to the streets, a scene that was duplicated in every city in the United States. And although the celebrants milled throughout the downtown district, most of them spent V-J Day [and night] at the corner of Hollywood and Vine at one time or another. There was a total disregard for traffic lights, and pedestrians took over the city's thoroughfares.

Above and right: Don the Beachcomber's, on McCadden, between Yucca and Hollywood Boulevard, is still a very popular spot to filmland celebrities, and is world famous for its invention and introduction of the Zombie Cocktail. The photograph above was taken in 1946; the one at right, in 1949.

Tourists and residents crowd the intersection of Hollywood and Vine to witness the unveiling of radio station KFWB's lighted newsboard, which was attached to the northwest corner of the Hollywood Taft Building. The crowd was entertained by Marie Wilson and Ken Murray, with music by Tommy Dorsey; 1946.

years, years of turmoil. Even during the war years, all was not harmony and peace in the entertainment industry. Divisions between people on different ends of the economic and political spectra were acute, although subdued during the war years to maximize support for the anti-Fascist fight.

But in late 1945, entertainment industry workers divided over unionism and politics. The ensuing battles dampened the spirits not only of the industry, but also of the Hollywood community.

Workers were joining unions in large numbers to maximize their benefits in the rich industry. Celebrities and studio executives made tons of money, and the "unsung heroes" behind the stage and screen sought a more equitable share of the enormous profits. How to accomplish this was not

evident to all. Some preferred to bargain on their own; others wanted to maintain craft unions; and still others thought that industry-wide unions would best benefit the industry's majority.

The International Alliance of Theatrical Stage Employees [IATSE] had been around the longest, since the 1920s, when it organized movie projectionists across the nation. Some workers felt its approach to union strategy was an old closed-shop attitude that kept many out of the union, while enhancing the lot of the few. Many workers wanted a broader union. Some of them were left-leaning in their political and economic views of the world; some were Communists; others were apolitical social reformers. Some were just interested in improving their economic well-being.

Economic divisions were exacerbated by the coming cold war between the war allies, the Soviet Union, and the United States. The differences were numerous: market economy vs. a controlled planned one; an open political tradition vs. a closed one; and both nations moved in the world as competing geopolitical controlling forces.

The U.S. Congress passed a law in 1938 creating the House Committee on Un-American Activities [HUAC], instructing it to investigate any activity deemed "un-American." There were loud voices against a law probing political thought, and there were boisterous advocates as well. They believed the nation was weakened by leftists who allegedly owed political allegiance to the Soviet Union. Others viewed the law as pernicious, illegal on its face because it prohibited First Amendment guarantees to free political ideas and associations.

Just before the U.S. got into World War II, Congress passed several laws forbidding Communists to hold certain employment; loyalty acts were passed forcing persons to swear they were not

Above: The Pilgrimage Play Theatre, nestled in the foothills of Cahuenga Pass, 1947.
Left: A Red Car approaches the Barham Boulevard underpass in the Cahuenga Pass; the Red Car's roadbed now lies beneath the Hollywood Freeway; photo, 1947.

Above: The experimental
mobile equipment of
Station W6XYZ, the
forerunner of KTLA,
Channel Five. Below:
Tom Breneman's
Restaurant, which was
located at 1525 Vine, was
the site from which
Breneman's network
radio show, *Breakfast in
Hollywood*, was
broadcast. Photo, 1947.

Above: The finale at a performance of the long running *Ken Murray's Blackouts* [1947]; 20s and 30s stage and film star Jack Mulhall is center stage [to right of and linking arms with an unidentified woman]; the backdrop is of Hollywood and Vine, featuring the Taft Building and the Brown Derby. Right: Outside the theater; this was formerly the Hollywood Playhouse Theatre, but took the name El Capitan in 1942 when the original El Capitan [on Hollywood Boulevard] changed its name to The Paramount; photo, 1947. Opposite page: Ken Murray and Marie Wilson on stage at the *Blackouts*; photo, 1949.

Top: Gilmore Field, at Beverly Boulevard and Fairfax Avenue, where the Hollywood Stars baseball team played; the site is now occupied by CBS Television City; photo, 1948. Above: Gilmore Stadium, which was next to Gilmore Field, seated 18,000 and was the birthplace of midget auto racing as a national sport; photo, 1947. Left: The Hitching Post Theater featured Saturday western matinees, but one had to check his cap pistol in the lobby; photo, 1948. Opposite page: Sid Grauman and actress Anne Baxter watch as Gregory Peck adds his name to the forecourt of Grauman's Chinese Theater; photo, 1949.

Communists. These efforts were sharply curtailed during the anti-Nazi war, but resumed in 1946. By 1947, the highly visible Hollywood industry was met with congressional hearings into the loyalty of nineteen Hollywood writers, directors, and actors.

HUAC maintained that Communists had "infiltrated the Hollywood industry and were producing subversive films." Many of those thought to be "subversive" were those anti-Fascist films of the war, such as *Thirty Seconds over Tokyo*, and *Mission to Moscow*. Yet, HUAC never named what films it considered "subversive." It simply denounced people whom it knew or presumed to be social activists.

Movie studio owners offered to help the committee by discharging and preventing from gaining Hollywood employment anyone not cooperating, anyone who failed to name names or who refused to sign loyalty statements prohibiting political acts.

Ten of the first nineteen subpoenaed before HUAC eventually were convicted of contempt, and when the U.S. Supreme Court refused to hear the case, they went to jail. A sweep of political leftists spread across the country. By the early 1950s,

Above: The Samuel Goldwyn Studios, at Santa Monica Blvd. and Formosa, 1949. Built in 1919 and occupied by Jesse Hampton, it later became the Pickford-Fairbanks Studio in 1922, and was renamed United Artists in 1927. Opposite: The Hollywood Hotel, almost fifty years after its opening; photograph, 1949.

some 400 Hollywood writers, actors, and directors were blacklisted.

After this HUAC success, Senator Joseph McCarthy mounted his attack against the Department of State and eventually the Pentagon. For the next four years, the nation was engulfed in accusations, in hysteria, and in war in Korea. Most people grew weary of war and wanted to get on with peace and economic prosperity. Most people in the Hollywood community felt that way, but also felt the fear. Teachers at the local high school were fired for their beliefs or for refusing to sign loyalty oaths.

Many of those blacklisted didn't work in Hollywood again for fifteen or more years. One star survived by raising flowers; another by waiting tables in an Arizona hotel. Some writers were able to get occasional writing jobs for one-tenth their worth and by using pseudonyms. Once the blacklist was broken, in the mid-1960s, some who

had been spurned became heroes. Whichever side one may have taken in those years, they were fearful times, yet, ironically, economically prosperous for many Americans.

Hollywood's identity as a bedroom community with a thriving retail business district changed after the Second World War, when the San Fernando Valley, once an area of stars' country ranches and working farms, was subdivided into housing tracts and developed for growth as a suburban area. The valley boomed in the early 1950s, taking thousands of Hollywood-born young parents out of the city.

The population increase in the valley placed additional pressure on the already congested Cahuenga Avenue, which was the primary access to and from downtown Los Angeles. Consisting of two lanes in each direction, with streetcar tracks down the center, the road cut through the busy streets of Hollywood and Echo Park. To alleviate these traffic problems, the state allocated $55 million for construction of the Hollywood Freeway. The three-phase construction of the ten-mile thoroughfare began in 1947. Its first phase opened in

October 1951; the second in March 1953; and it was completed in 1954.

Yet freeway growth was not entirely well received. Many residents didn't want the Red Cars eliminated. As one old-timer put it, "The Red Cars were good public transportation. Sure, they were slow and noisy, but they kept us together and got us where we wanted to go."

But progress brought Hollywood the freeways and a massive influx of new humanity. Although the friendly, residential family community began to change with the new people, much of Hollywood's community spirit remained. Churches and civic clubs continued to grow.

Live Entertainment and Music

Hollywood's Sunset Strip was transformed from farmland and bridle paths to a playground for stars in the 1930s. Focal point of nightclub activity, the strip's best-known clubs were the Trocadero Cafe, the Mocambo, and Ciro's.

Opened in 1934, the Trocadero Cafe, owned

Top: The KTLA Studio Theatre at Melrose and Van Ness, 1951. Bottom: The Mutual Don Lee Broadcasting System, 1951; today it's the ABC Vine Street Theatre. Opposite page: Bette Davis adds her famous name and prints to the Chinese forecourt, 1950.

by the *Hollywood Reporter* publisher W.R. Wilkerson, became a nightspot for celebrities, residents and curious tourists. Packed crowds danced, dined, and were entertained by stars, such as Judy Garland, Mary Martin, Martha Raye, Tony Martin, and Deanna Durbin. A fire completely gutted the club in 1936 but it reopened under new management the following year. The "Troc" continued to be one of Hollywood's most celebrated nightspots until it closed in 1946.

Close to the Trocadero, the Mocambo opened in 1939, at 8588 Sunset Boulevard. Owner Charles Morrison turned it into a favorite "haunt" for members of the movie colony. The flashiest stars relaxed here and were entertained by some of the nation's finest performers, including Edith Piaf, Billy Daniels, and Lena Horne. In 1958, shortly after Morrison's death, the club closed.

Three years after the fire at his first club, Wilkerson opened another club two blocks from his former Trocadero. Ciro's didn't get off to a great start and folded after three years. But, under new management, it soon became one of the most famous Hollywood hotspots. Owner Herman Hover remodeled, turning the club into one of the largest and most lavish. It soon became packed nightly, as audiences listened and watched Jerry Lewis, Dean Martin, Sophie Tucker, Sammy Davis Jr., Peggy Lee, Maurice Chevalier, and Liberace. Eartha Kitt made her nightclub debut at the famous Ciro's. With the increasing popularity of the Las Vegas shows, Hollywood's nightclubs found it impossible to compete with the enormous salaries paid entertainers by the gambling capital of the world. After more than fifteen years of entertaining Hollywood's "Who's Who," Ciro's went out of business in the late 1950s. Today, Ciro's is the Comedy Store, a workshop-type nightclub for stand-up comedians, owned by Mitzi Shore.

One of New York's most popular shows was Earl Carroll's *Vanities* revue. The production, which ran from 1923 to 1936, was actually a refined burlesque show and was continuously raided by the police. Closing and reopening began to take its financial toll. With his fortune ebbing because of high court and production costs, Earl Carroll left New York.

After arriving in Hollywood in 1936 and finding sufficient financial backing, he opened the Earl Carroll Theater at Sunset Boulevard and Argyle Street on December 26, 1938. Opening night was one of the most dazzling events Hollywood had ever seen. Countless celebrities and professional leaders attended the colorful premiere, while hundreds of spectators stood outside the theater to watch their favorite stars drive up to the entrance. The star-studded pageant included such personalities as Marlene Dietrich, Delores Del Rio, Richard Barthelmess, Tyrone Power, Clark Gable, Carole Lombard, Robert Taylor, and Errol Flynn. The production, which emphasized the beauty of the partially clad female form, boasted a cast of sixty showgirls. Carroll, who meticulously selected

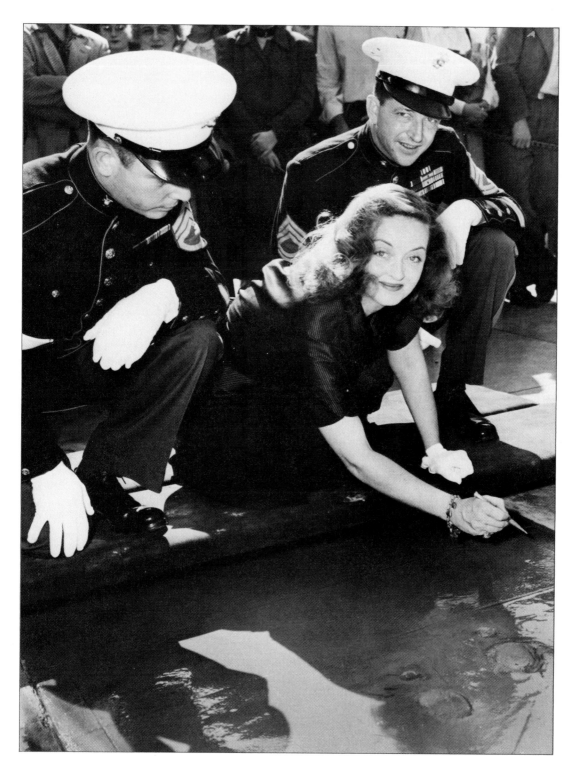

each of the cast members, adopted the slogan, "Through these doors pass the most beautiful girls in the world." This proclamation was later made in neon lights outside the theater. The show, headed by Beryl Wallace, became an immediate success and later developed such personalities as Yvonne DeCarlo, Jean Wallace, Sheree North, and Marie MacDonald.

Carroll's colossal theater, which accommodated 1,160 customers, was lit by 10,000 neon tubes, which were suspended from a patent-leather ceiling. With an elevated revolving stage, there was not a bad seat in the house. For $2.50—later the tab was raised to $3.50—the customer received a fine dinner, danced, and witnessed one of the most spectacular and lavish revues in show business history.

Slightly less than a decade after it was started,

Above: The section of Hollywood Freeway through Cahuenga Pass nears completion; street at left is Highland; street at right is Cahuenga. Opposite page: W6XYZ gives its viewers a preview of how it will work. Only one thing is missing from the station's model—about 2,000 more model cars; photos taken in 1952.

the production came to a tragic end when Earl Carroll and Beryl Wallace were killed in an airplane accident in Pennsylvania on June 17, 1948.

For five years after Carroll's untimely death, the Earl Carroll Theater was operated by various promoters trying vainly to make it a success. It was not until Frank Sennes took it over in 1953, that it again became the center of night-life gaiety in Hollywood. An extensive remodeling campaign was undertaken which included expanding the seating capacity to 1,250, making the Moulin Rouge the largest theater-restaurant in the world.

From the beginning, Sennes was dedicated to the policy of providing the finest stage entertain-

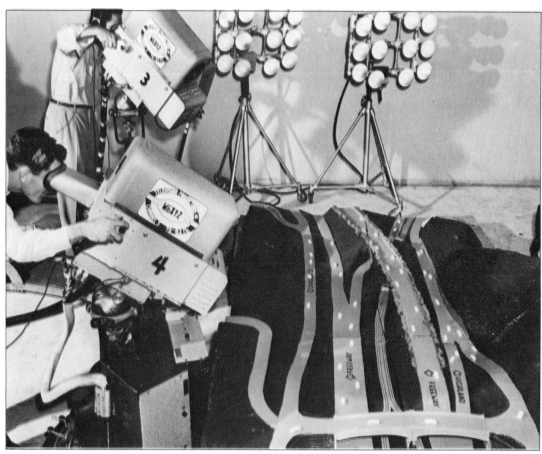

ment available. During the seven years of its illustrious existence, the Moulin Rouge presented
countless outstanding personalities such as Peggy
Lee, Ella Fitzgerald, Billy Daniels, Dean Martin,
Dennis Day, the Mills Brothers, Anna Maria Alber-
ghetti, Frankie Laine, Johnnie Ray, and Mr. Show-
man himself, Liberace. In addition to the star head-
liners, the show assembled more than 100 beautiful
singers and dancers, who paraded around the large
stage in costumes costing thousands of dollars.

The success that the Moulin Rouge experienced was due, in part, to what Sennes called his
"package deal." For just $5.50, the customer re-
ceived a complete, full-course deluxe dinner,
danced to a fine orchestra, and watched top entertainers perform. Sunday afternoons were devoted
to a family matinee, which featured a kiddie circus,
complete with clowns, balloons and toys. Beginning in 1955, the daytime television show "Queen
For a Day," starring host, Jack Bailey, was broadcast

from the Moulin Rouge.

By the late 1950s, Sennes found it increasingly difficult to attract top-name entertainers, because of his inability to compete with the high salaries being paid by Las Vegas. Recognizing the
enormous potential and opportunity that Las
Vegas had to offer, he closed the Moulin Rouge in
1960 and began producing shows in the gambling
capital of the United States. The theater has since
been renamed The Aquarius, and is rented out for
legitimate stage presentations.

Across the street from Earl Carroll's, the
Hollywood Palladium opened its doors on October
31, 1940, exactly four months after luscious Lana
Turner, with a silver shovel, "starred" in the
ground-breaking ceremony. The famous auditorium has played host to more than 38 million
people, including a galaxy of famous entertainment stars who constitute a veritable "Who's Who"
of the film and television capital of the world: Judy

Above: Looking east from Whitley on Hollywood Boulevard during the holidays, 1951.
Left: The Farmers Market at Third and Fairfax, 1952.
Opposite page: The dedication ceremony for the last link in the Hollywood Freeway that will connect Los Angeles with the San Fernando Valley; 1953.

Garland, Betty Grable, Harry James, Tommy and Jimmy Dorsey, Doris Day, Les Brown, Marilyn Monroe, Martha Raye, Peggy Lee, Benny Goodman, Freddy Martin, Gene Krupa, Glenn Miller—and the list goes on and on.

The Hollywood Palladium, constructed at a cost of $1,600,000, was the dream child of Norman Chandler, publisher of the *Los Angeles Times* and owner of the property. Located on Sunset Boulevard, and occupying the entire block from Argyle to El Centro, the Palladium has entertained five United States presidents: Harry S. Truman, Dwight D. Eisenhower, John F. Kennedy, Lyndon B. Johnson, and Richard M. Nixon.

In July 1961, television producer Don Fedder-son, in concert with Sam J. Lutz, assumed management and operation of the Palladium, and forthwith signed America's most noted television bandleader, Lawrence Welk, to appear there weekly. For more than fifteen years the maestro appeared some twenty-five Saturdays a year, playing his popular music for thousands of Los Angeles admirers. Today the Palladium continues to host sales meetings, trade shows, and countless other events.

Among Hollywood's hotspots, one of the biggest and flashiest was the Florentine Gardens, located at 5955 Hollywood Boulevard. Even in a community never noted for modest standards, it was colossal. Not highly popular with most movie celebrities who preferred the exclusive intimacy of

such places as Ciro's, the Trocadero and the Mocambo, the noisy barnlike club went in for quantity rather than quality. It managed to pack its 500 seats almost nightly. The inducement was a floor show that was a mixture of excitement, sex, and audience participation. Nils Thor Granlund staged the shows. In a large measure, the success of the gardens was due to the fact that people will pay well for the privilege of watching tall, gorgeous showgirls parade around in various stages of undress. Aside from the beautiful girls, a variety of acts entertained the customers. The Flying Herzogs was a trapeze circus act that held Florentine Gardens audiences in suspense, when they performed high above the stage floor. In addition, big-name entertainers like Paul Whiteman and his orchestra, Sophie Tucker, Harry Richman and his band, Willie Howard, the Mills Brothers, and Yvonne DeCarlo appeared at the club.

During the war, servicemen were admitted without charge and were seated in a special reserved section to watch the show. The Florentine

Gardens filed bankruptcy in 1948; however, under new management, it continued as a restaurant, using the same name, Florentine Gardens, until it finally went out of business in 1954.

Hollywood had many other clubs and restaurants in the heyday of the Thirties and Forties. The Clover Club, raided often for gambling and liquor violations, closed just before the war. Others, off the strip, included the plush It Cafe, at 1637 Vine Street, named for its owner, silent screen star Clara Bow; around the corner, at 6160 Hollywood Boulevard, was The Toad in the Hole, a favorite with Hollywood socialites; there were also Al Levy's Tavern on Vine, Cafe Lamaze at 9039 Sunset Boulevard, and the still in operation Tick Tock Tea Room at 1716 North Cahuenga Avenue.

Another popular Hollywood source of "live" entertainment was sports, especially baseball. In 1938, Robert Cobb, who owned the Brown Derby restaurant, and Victor Ford Collins engineered the acquisition of the San Francisco Mission baseball team [formerly the Vernon Tigers]. Upon moving

HELEN HAYES IN WHAT EVERY WOMAN KNOWS WITH KENT SMITH

HUNTINGTON HARTFORD THEATRE

Left: Built in the mid-twenties, the old Vine Street Theatre reverted to its legitimate ways when it was given a face lift and reopened as the Huntington Hartford Theatre in 1954. For twenty-five years, the Huntington Hartford has brought to Hollywood many of the world's finest plays. Opposite page: The premiere of *The Robe* at Grauman's Chinese Theatre, 1953.

to Los Angeles, the ball club changed its name to the Hollywood Stars, and joined the Pacific Coast League.

Once in the southland, the Stars played at Wrigley Field. Later, they moved to Gilmore Field [next to Gilmore Stadium and the present site of CBS Television]. In 1949, Fred Haney took over the managerial reins of the club and harvested two pennants. Bobby Bragan followed Haney and guided the Stars to another pennant. The club's ownership list reads like a Hollywood "Who's Who": George Burns, Gracie Allen, Gary Cooper, Cecil B. DeMille, Walt Disney, William Frawley, George Stevens, and Bing Crosby.

Los Angeles' acquisition of the Brooklyn Dodgers meant the ruin of the Pacific Coast League. The Hollywood Stars played their last game in front of 6,354 spectators, on September 5, 1957.

Hollywood's famous outdoor amphitheater, the Hollywood Bowl, was experiencing serious financial difficulties in 1951. Attendance was so small, audiences literally rattled around the enormous bowl. The board of directors appointed Dorothy Buffum Chandler, wife of *Los Angeles Times'* publisher, to head reorganization. She raised the necessary funds to rescue the bowl and became its president in 1954. It remains today a major center of entertainment life for Hollywood residents and thousands of tourists.

The beginning of the "Golden Age of Radio"

took place when the country was in the throes of the Great Depression during the early 1930s. Sensing that radio was in a growth cycle, Glenn Wallichs opened a small shop on Ivar Avenue, just south of Hollywood Boulevard, to sell and service radios for home and automobiles. He called his new store Music City, and during the ensuing years, widely expanded the range of merchandise. By 1940, expansion dictated the need for larger quarters. Music City moved into a building on the northwest corner of Sunset and Vine, a location they continued to occupy for almost forty years. Two years later, in 1942, they began to sell records, and they were the first music store to introduce the self-service concept, the first to use record browser racks, and the first to set up demonstration rooms so that their customers could listen to the records that they planned to purchase. During the same year, Glenn Wallichs joined with Johnny Mercer and Buddy DeSylva to form Capital Records Company. This new business required most of Wallichs' time, so in 1949, he sold controlling interest in Music City to his brother, Clyde, who renamed it Clyde Wallichs Music City. Years later, the merchandise was expanded to include sheet music, musical instruments, pianos, organs, and phonographs, thus making it one of the largest and most complete music stores in the world. After operating for many years as Hollywood's music center, Wallichs Music City went out of business in 1978, thus becoming part of Hollywood's fabulous past.

Glenn Wallichs concentrated his energies on building Capitol Records, a classic saga of successful showmanship and business acumen. Songwriter Johnny Mercer felt that his tunes, and those of others, weren't getting proper showcasing on discs. Wallichs felt the need to expand into something more substantial. Together, and with Buddy De-Sylva, executive producer at Paramount Pictures, they started a new company, Liberty Records, which soon changed its name to Capitol Records. The three had their fingers on the pulse of the mass music-listening audience. Two numbers on the first release, "Cow-Cow Boogie," by Ella Mae Morse and Freddie Slack, and "Strip Polka," sung by Mercer, became the nation's top record hits.

From the start, Capitol strayed from typical recording company behavior by cooperating fully with radio disc jockeys, profiding them with sample records of each release. This has since become standard industry practice.

Capitol Records first operated out of a small storefront in the Music City building at Sunset and Vine. But, by 1954, larger facilities were needed, and construction on a new home for Capitol was begun. For two years, Hollywood residents watched the mysterious new building reach higher and higher until, in 1956, the world's first circular office building was completed. Its thirteen-story structure remains a Hollywood landmark.

Leading the way to success throughout Capitol's history has been its impressive roster of performers, including Nat "King" Cole, Jo Stafford, Margaret Whiting, Stan Kenton, Peggy Lee, Les Paul, Mary Ford, Frank Sinatra, Dean Martin, Nelson Riddle, and Kay Starr.

The Tube Comes to Hollywood

The movie industry's most prosperous and glamorous period spanned the Thirties and Forties,

Above: A view of the NBC radio and television complex on the corner of Sunset and Vine, with parking lot on the north side. The dark areas beside the parking lot [southeast corner of Vine and Selma] mark the approximate site of the barn where Cecil B. DeMille had his first motion picture production office in 1913. The large building [top right] is the Hollywood Palladium; 1954.

when walled-studio empires governed huge stables of actors, directors, producers, writers, and technicians, who produced about 750 films a year [compared with today's major-studio output of less than 200 a year]. But by 1948, the industry was staggering from a number of blows—some self-inflicted. Theater attendance was down forty-five percent from war-time box-office highs. The specter of empty seats and closing theaters panicked the movie moguls, who began exploiting gimmicks to win back audiences: wide screen, stereophonic sound, three dimensions, and even giveaway premiums, such as dishes—to no avail. Regardless of whether the blows that rocked the industry were fair or foul, and regardless of their origin, it's generally conceded that the blow that brought the industry to its knees came from a brash, neophyte contender for the national heavyweight entertainment crown—television.

From 1946 to 1951, the number of television sets in American homes increased from an estimated 10,000 to more than 12 million, hastening the demise of neighborhood movie houses and eliciting the wrath of movie people for wrecking such havoc on their industry. But the movie industry had only itself to blame; it didn't take television seriously, and it had been given ample time to do so. Television wasn't exactly a new kid on

Television and radio personality Jack Bailey hosts the burial of a Hollywood time capsule [1954] at the corner of Sunset and Vine; unfortunately, water ruined all the artifacts it contained.

the block. In fact, the third television station established in Hollywood was owned and operated by the Paramount Picture Corporation.

The "new" medium actually took root in Hollywood during the depression. It was just two days before Christmas in 1931 when the Don Lee station—then known as W6XAO—went on the air with a daily program of old motion picture films. The station gave its first public demonstration three years later, and thousands flocked to witness the 300-line, twenty-four-frame system developed by television pioneer Harry R. Lubcke.

By the early Forties, the Don Lee group had constructed a modern facility atop Mount Cahuenga, just above the HOLLYWOODLAND sign; the new plant was the first to be designed specifically for television. In the Fifties, the Don Lee station was purchased by CBS.

Eight years after W6XAO went on the air,

Earle C. Anthony, a wealthy businessman and successful Packard car dealer, received permission to erect a television broadcasting station, using the call letters KECA. Anthony operated the station for four years before selling it to ABC. In 1948, ABC bought the 23-acre Warner Brothers lot at Prospect and Talmadge Avenues. Conversion to television transmission began at once, and on September 16, 1949, the gates were opened to what was then the world's largest television plant, hous-

ing the studios and general administrative headquarters for ABC on the Pacific Coast. The KECA call letters were changed to KABC in 1953, and the station remains the network's local outlet.

In 1939, Klaus Landsberg came to Hollywood and established an experimental television station for Paramount Pictures Corporation, with the call letters W6XYZ. Since there were only a few television sets in all of California at the time, the station had no ratings worries and, for the first seven

years, broadcast nothing but civil defense programs, parades, variety shows, and World War II bulletins, all the while headquartered in a small building on the Paramount lot at Melrose and Bronson. On January 22, 1947, the station changed its call letters to KTLA and became the first commercial station west of Chicago. The number of television receivers in Los Angeles at the time was estimated at 350.

KTLA began commercial broadcasting that

Above: Sunset and Vine, looking north on Vine Street, 1954. ABC occupied what is today the TAV Celebrity Theatre; Coffee Dan's was going strong; Capitol Records was still occupying space in Wallachs' Music City building—though the ground breaking ceremony had just taken place for its new, circular tower across from the Hollywood Palace—NBC was still on the corner, and the Plaza was still a hotel where stars gathered.

Top: Earl Carroll had opened the doors to his new theater on December 26, 1938. And just one day short of fifteen years later, on December 25, 1953, the doors were opened again as Frank Sennes' Moulin Rouge. Like Carroll, Sennes brought the entertainment industry's finest stars to the theater's stage and offered the West Coast's best entertainment package until the stars' skyrocketing salaries forced him to close in 1960. Above: Ciro's was one of the most popular night clubs in Hollywood's history; now it's occupied by the popular Comedy Store; 1953.

Top: Johnny Grant, Jack Benny, and Danny Kaye at the popular Mocambo, 1955. Left: The lobby of the Mocambo; through the kiosk-like door and to the right lay the main room; directly in front, as the sign indicates, was the women's restroom. Above: Patrons line up to see Eartha Kitt, who was making her first West Coast appearance since her Broadway hit, *New Faces of 1952.* The Mocambo was opened at 8588 Sunset Boulevard by Charlie Morrison in 1939, and gained more than a measure of world renown. It closed in 1958, shortly after Mr. Morrison's death.

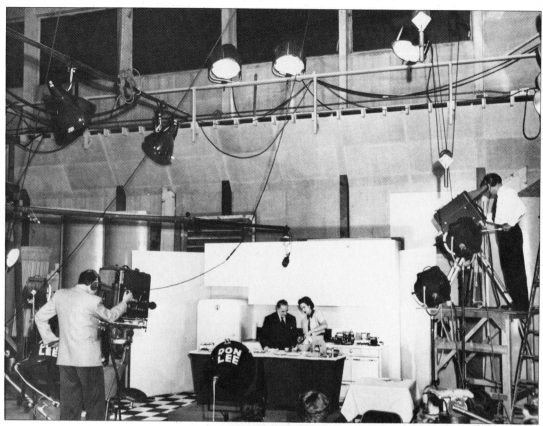

Above: The broadcast of a cooking program at the Don Lee Station on Vine Street [now ABC Vine Street Theatre]; such shows were easy to produce and numerous in the early days; photo, 1953. Right: Rehearsals take place in the background as the live camera focuses on a test pattern; in those days, test patterns were broadcast more hours than regular programming; photo, 1954. Opposite, top: Even watching people's backs during election night drew audiences in television's infancy; this is CBS on election night, 1956, and the Eisenhower-Nixon ticket won its second term. Opposite, bottom: a view from the engineer's booth, CBS, 1955.

year with the historic words: "This is KTLA, formerly W6XYZ Television, Los Angeles, broadcasting on Channel Five. Good Evening, everyone." The emcee for Hollywood's first commercial television program? None other than Bob Hope. Cecil B. DeMille opened the program, which also featured Dorothy Lamour, William Bendix, Ann Rutherford, Peter Lind Hayes, the Rhythmaires, William Demarest, the DeCastro Sisters, and Jerry Colonna.

Aside from the entertainment brought into one's own home, television had the potential of outstripping other news media with live and immediate news coverage in sound and pictures. This potential was amply demonstrated on April 8, 1949, when three-year-old Kathy Fiscus fell into a 230-foot abandoned water well while playing in a vacant lot. Over 5,000 spectators were drawn to the scene as KTLA offered uninterrupted on-the-scene coverage by newscaster Bill Welsh for twenty-eight hours, until the tragic end. The zenith

Opposite page: A premiere at the Paramount Theatre, formerly the El Capitan, on Hollywood Boulevard, 1956. Above: An era ended when, in 1956, the Hollywood Hotel couldn't meet safety and building standards and had to be razed; it opened in 1903.

of such coverage would occur twenty years later as we watched Edwin "Buzz" Aldrin and Neil Armstrong walk on the surface of the moon—live, a quarter-million miles from earth!

As television grew in popularity, KTLA grew as well. In 1955, the station was relocated by Paramount Pictures Corporation to the old Warner Brothers Studio lot on Sunset Boulevard, which it had purchased in 1942. Paramount continued operating KTLA until it sold its license and television facilities to Golden West Broadcasters on May 13, 1964. In 1967, Golden West purchased the entire 10-acre site from Paramount. The latest addition to the lot came in June 1968 when Golden West moved KMPC, their AM radio station, to 5858 Sunset Boulevard, on the northern end of the property.

A view of the flower fields on Los Feliz Boulevard, just east of Griffith Park's Ferndale, before it was subdivided; photo, 1958.

Station KLAC, Channel 13, began broadcasting in September 1948 with a telecast of the USC-Utah football game. During the Fifties, the call letters were changed to KCOP, and it was in their studios—still located on La Brea Avenue—that such personalities as Del Moore, Betty White, and Liberace first performed on television.

KTTV, Channel 11, began in more modest fashion, from the top floor of the Bekins Building, near Melrose and Highland. But they weren't at all inhibited by their spartan facilities. On New Year's Day, 1949, they launched their first project: on-the-spot coverage of the Tournament of Roses Parade. Their "Studio" in the Bekins Building would be a television producer's nightmare today; it had eight-foot ceilings, and was so cramped that the sets had to be built back-to-back for shows that aired live. Acoustics were terrible and soundproofing impossible. Many of their fine shows, like "Wheeler and Rourke," "The Red Nichols Show," and "Matt Dennis' Music Shop" often included the

unscheduled sounds of passing fire engines and low-flying planes. Sign-on time was between 6:30 P.M. and 7:00 P.M., and the length of a typical broadcast day was only four or five hours. Walter Carl was KTTV's first newscaster, and he would have amazed today's reporters with his ability to memorize the entire news script prior to going on the air.

Within the year, KTTV moved to a studio on Melrose Avenue. Locally popular shows such as "Happy Hangs His Hat," with Tom Hattan, and the Emmy-winning Mike Stokey's "Pantomine Quiz" aired from the Melrose Avenue studios. Shortly thereafter, the station moved again, this time to the former El Patio Theater. From there were broadcast such shows as "At Home With the Meakins," "The Freddy Martin Show" featuring singer Merv Griffin and his smash hit "I've Got A Lovely Bunch of Coconuts" and last but by no means least, "The

Buster Keaton Show."

In 1952, KTTV's broadcast facility was moved to its present location at Sunset Boulevard and Van Ness Avenue, and brought to local audiences such well-known television programs as "You Asked for It," "The Tom Duggan Show," "The Pamela Mason Show," and such broadcasters as George Putnam, Alex Drier, Jack Latham, and Bill Welsh.

Until its acquisition in 1963 by Metromedia Incorporated, KTTV had been a subsidiary of the Times-Mirror Company. Metromedia brought to KTTV the added dimension of syndication and, combined with the corporation's other stations, many of the characteristics of a network operation.

Meanwhile, NBC's huge radio complex at Sunset and Vine converted partially to television transmission and made its debut on January 16, 1949 as station KNBH. It was the first station to broadcast professional football games and the first

Actress Virginia Mayo taps a silver spike into a star at the corner of Hollywood Boulevard and Argyle to kick off a Hollywood Boulevard face-lifting program. Standing with Miss Mayo are E.M. Stuart, Harry M. Sugarman, and Otto K. Olesen; 1956.

to do a microwave relay of a live pro game from San Francisco. Its call letters were changed in 1954 to KRCA, and again in 1962 to KNBC.

CBS entered the competition in a big way. After purchasing Hollywood's first television station, W6XAO, in the Fifties, it constructed a 35-acre complex at Beverly and Fairfax [former site of Gilmore Stadium] in 1952. Known as CBS Television City, the complex was designed solely for television and was an initiator of the switch from live programming to the filmed product.

The Public Broadcasting System, PBS, was operating in the mid-Fifties in Los Angeles, but it didn't make its Hollywood debut until the early Sixties. Operated by Community Television of

Comedian Red Skelton in the Santa Claus Lane Parade, 1956.

Southern California, KCET went on the air in 1964 from studios at 1313 North Vine. Currently the third largest noncommercial public television station in the country—and the only one to broadcast around the clock, five days a week—KCET moved in 1970 to one of Hollywood's most famous landmark studios at 4401 Sunset [since 1912, the home of eleven motion picture companies, including Lubin, Essanay, Kalem, Monogram, and Allied Artists].

Thus, by the mid-Fifties, television had risen full-faced to eclipse the Hollywood movie industry. They were dark days. Contract players were cut from the studio payrolls; sound stages went black; back lots fell into disrepair and were given up to weeds. After forty triumphant years Hollywood's dream merchants were faced with a nightmarish reality. Doomsters listened for the death rattle to break the silence. But it didn't come.

The ingenious showmen who had built the industry were resourceful still. No sooner had the transcontinental video cable been completed than Hollywood won its share of live network shows. Then, as television gained the lion's share of the nation's advertising budgets and it became popular to put shows on film, Hollywood was ready to corner the market.

By the end of the Fifties, more sound stages were being employed for television films than for theatrical movies. Nearly every studio in Hollywood was keeping its stages busy. And though it was little consolation to theater owners across the nation, Hollywood had made the transition to television, and was again active and prospering.

Hollywood:
In the Eye of the Beholder

Tourism plays a major role in Hollywood's economy. And even the entertainment industry's

One of the first eight stars to be set in the Walk of Fame was that of Joanne Woodward in 1958; she's shown polishing her star, which is located on Hollywood Boulevard at Highland Avenue.

darkest days didn't diminish the numbers of tourists who visited Hollywood. Each year they come by the millions from all parts of the world, and return home as minor celebrities themselves for having seen the movie mecca and perhaps a celebrity or two. But there is disappointment, too, which is inevitable when one comes in search of the image that is Hollywood, the concept in the mind's eye.

The problem with concepts and images is that they have no finite existence, and can be explored only through symbols. Up to the mid-Fifties, there were very few symbols that the average tourist could utilize to invoke the image. What they found instead was a town on the skids, decaying as quickly as were the sets on the back lots of its major studios. They found a town much like any other town, with real and ordinary people, a town in which no concerted effort had been made to give substance to the image. There was no glamor, no streets paved with gold—yet.

Prior to the mid-Fifties, two time capsules had been placed beneath Hollywood's sidewalks. The one embedded on the corner of Hollywood and Vine contained the megaphone that Cecil B. De-Mille used in directing *The Squaw Man*, one of Will Roger's favorite lariats, a pipe from Bing Crosby's collection and his gold millionth record of "Silent Night," a favorite green fedora from Jimmy Durante, two self-portrait sketches of John Barrymore in the role of Svengali, Harold Lloyd's only pair of glassless glasses, and a frontier-model revolver used by John Wayne in his early westerns.

Two years earlier, a capsule had been placed at the corner of Sunset and Vine, in front of NBC's radio studio, to commemorate Hollywood's fiftieth anniversary. It contained a record from Jack Benney's radio broadcast, a script from the "I Love Lucy" TV show, a fiftieth anniversary issue of the *Citizen News*—then Hollywood's daily newspaper—and special issues of the trades—*The Hollywood Reporter* and *Daily Variety*. But ten years later, when NBC was razed, the capsule was found to contain water because it hadn't been hermetically sealed; the artifacts were ruined.

But something more than time capsules was needed, and in the mid-Fifties the Hollywood Chamber of Commerce took a long, hard look at its city and spearheaded a glamorization program, including a plan that would pay tribute to the talented artists who created and perpetrated the aura that has made Hollywood world famous. The plan called for installing a sidewalk to be called The Walk of Fame, made of charcoal terrazzo squares embedded with coral terrazzo stars outlined in brass. Inside each star was to be an artist's name, also in brass. A new street-lighting system, with lamps ten times more powerful than those in use, and the planting of new trees were included in the plan.

In order to carry out the project, the Hollywood Improvement Association was formed and headed by Harry M. Sugarman. Under the association's direction, the Hollywood Assessment District was established, which raised $1,250,000 by assessing property owners along the Walk of Fame eighty-five dollars per front foot.

The first eight stars were dedicated in September 1958 and placed in the sidewalk on the northwest corner of Hollywood Boulevard and Highland Avenue. They were installed several months prior to the official 1960 Walk of Fame ground-breaking, so as to be ready when the new, twelve-story First Federal Savings of Hollywood Building was completed in January 1959. The eight film notables who bear the distinction of being the first to have their names placed in the Hollywood Walk of Fame are Preston Foster, Joanne Woodward, Ernest Torrence, Olive Borden, Edward Sedgwick, Louise Fazenda, Ronald Coleman, and Burt Lancaster.

The official ground-breaking ceremonies were conducted on February 8, 1960, and when construction was completed sixteen months later, 1,558 entertainment industry luminaries were immortalized in the sidewalks of Hollywood Boulevard and Vine Street. Since then, the name of one star per month has been added to the famed walk, which will bring a total of 1,716 names by December 31, 1979.

Today, having one's name placed on the Walk of Fame is Hollywood's most coveted honor, and Hollywood citizens look forward with eager anticipation to each new dedication ceremony. The selection criteria is extensive, stressing public and peer recognition. Of the hundreds of nominations received annually, only a dozen are selected for installation each year.

Stars on the sidewalk are just part of the attraction to the tourists who pour into California by the millions. Tourism, apart from conventions, is California's third largest industry. Some two million tourists visited Hollywood in 1950; by 1962 that figure was five million, and in 1974 tourism in Hollywood had grown to 8.4 million visitors.

The tourists add millions of dollars to Hollywood's economy. A breakdown of how the traveler spends his dollar indicates that twenty percent goes for accommodations, twenty-five percent for food and beverages, twenty-five percent for transportation, twenty percent for entertainment, and five percent for Hollywood mementos.

But while Hollywood civic leaders grew more mindful of Hollywood as symbol in the Fifties, there was the reality of the finite Hollywood to deal with; "my town," with its churches, civic organizations, YMCA, temples, stores, parks, and schools. A city the size of Hollywood is difficult enough to administer even when its industry is stable and its inhabitants are permanently settled. But throw its industry in turmoil and begin a mass exodus to suburbia and you're courting disaster. The turbulent Sixties were at hand.

Part Four:
1960-1969

Hollywood wasn't a bad place to live the year Jack Kennedy was elected president. The sidewalks were being torn up for the Walk of Fame, but on Saturday nights it still took less time to walk Hollywood Boulevard from Highland to Vine than it did to drive. The Hollywood Hotel was gone, but the Roosevelt, Plaza, and Knickerbocker housed many entertainment luminaries. Searchlights still stroked the sky above the Chinese. The family could enjoy dinner and a movie without fear of felonious assault.

The boulevard was a playground for high schoolers on Friday and Saturday nights, but the kids' activities seemed more innocent and less consequential than kids' activities did later. "There were still car clubs back then," a 1960 graduate of Hollywood High School remembers. "The car to have was a '49 Olds 88 hydramatic coupe. We'd just cruise the boulevard and try to pick up girls."

Nor had the battlelines yet been drawn between young people and the police. "We had respect for the cops," says a 1960 Fairfax High alumnus. "*Boy*, did we have respect." Not that the police had to do much more with the under eighteen crowd than break up drag races and enforce the 10:00 P.M. curfew. "One night—I was about fifteen—I was drag racing down Bronson Avenue," our Hollywood High grad reminisced. "It was about eleven, and sure enough, here comes a cop. He took me to the station and called my folks, and while I was waiting for them, the cops showed me a bunch of kids with their heads bashed in from car accidents."

High schoolers would pile into Scrivner's and watch Art Laboe do a remote into KRLA. Or they'd stroll over to M'Goo's after a movie for some pizza and root beer. Impala convertibles, Chinese fire drills, and "backseat bingo" were the trappings of youth culture in 1960. *American Graffiti* with kleig lights.

Hollywood's population at the top of the Sixties was overwhelmingly Anglo and fairly evenly distributed by age groups, with about half the population in the thirty-to-sixty-five age range. It no longer contained as many wealthy people, except for a smattering in the hills, but its pockets of poverty were also few. It held a sizable transient population—the constant rotation of young people trying to get into the movies—but to a large extent it was still a community of normal families that shopped, worked, and attended school in the area.

Hollywood Boulevard could have been Main Street, USA, but unlike most main streets, it was lined with movie palaces and paved with brass-bound stars. Front-page items in the conservative, yet star-struck, *Hollywood Citizen News* would include a starlet's first baby or an actor's fourth marriage. The aura of Hollywood-as-Movieland soaked into every aspect of life there. "Stefanie Powers was in my homeroom," our Class of '60 representative remembers dreamily. And heaven knows who you could run into at Musso & Frank Grill. Hollywood was still the hub of the West's largest city—the glamour capital of the world.

But basic problems in the glamour capital had been brewing for years, and they began to make their full impact on the community during the early part of the Sixties. The cultural backbone of Hollywood, the film industry, whose output had declined steadily during the Fifties, entered the new decade with theatrical releases at an all-time low.

The studios' loss of their theater chains in 1948 and the enormous popularity of television made motion pictures less necessary as a mass medium. The film companies had been the logical generators of television programming, but they entered the medium too late to gain any control over its content; that power had passed to the networks. The studios became little more than renters of space to the television people, many of whom were former theatrical-film personnel who had been released from contracts five or ten years earlier.

Television bailed out the studios financially, but it did little for morale. In a 1960 article, "Visit to a Ghost Town," film historian Arthur Knight quotes a director who complains, "We have a wonderful instrument here. Technically, our studios are marvelously equipped, and our technicians are the best in the world. But these TV films—it's using a Stradivarius to play ragtime!"

The character of the theatrical-film business was also changing drastically. Studio heads no longer presided over private fiefdoms. Indepen-

dent producers and even actors formed their own companies and found themselves wielding unprecedented power on the lots; no longer could they be readily replaced by other contract personnel. The actors' and writers' strikes of early 1960 were only a symptom, not a cause, of the film companies dwindling product.

Rentals of space to television production became even more crucial as increasing numbers of filmmakers decided to shoot their films away from Hollywood, rejecting the sound stages for the realism of location settings—or Los Angeles for the cultural climate of New York or Europe. "They want to escape the supervision of executives who are more concerned with the account ledgers than with films," Knight wrote in 1960. "And they want to escape the closed-circuit system of big-studio production that, many of them feel, helped bring the industry to its present state...."

The major studios settled into the role of distribution depots—a symbol of decline not apparent to tourists.

The phenomena that caused Hollywood's rapid decline in the postwar era intensified during the Sixties. The San Fernando Valley continued to boom, and as regional shopping malls and suburban movie theaters sprang up, valley residents no longer needed to drive over the hill for goods, services, or entertainment. Community leaders in Hollywood saw "urbanization" as a remedy to the stagnation and decay that plagued the area.

The Hollywood Freeway, which provided easy access to the area from downtown and the valley, opened Hollywood as a prime location for office buildings. "Geographically, Hollywood is the hub of the Los Angeles area," explains real estate developer Arthur Kaplan, who built several office towers in Hollywood during the Sixties. "Once the freeway went through, it took fifteen to twenty minutes to get there from the valley and eight to ten minutes from downtown. A lawyer, say, with a case in court could be at civic center in ten minutes." A professional conducting business on the telephone could appreciate the fact that Hollywood exchanges provided a wider area of

Above: Construction of the Walk of Fame. Left: Actress Jayne Mansfield at the dedication of her star; both photographs, 1960.

nontoll calls than any other Los Angeles business district.

The firms of Kaplan and Black, Stanley Folb, and others erected a dozen high-rise office buildings during the Sixties. Led by the Los Angeles Federal Savings tower [1963], these structures include the RCA Building at Sunset and Wilcox, the Crocker Bank Building at Sunset and Cahuenga, and the United California Bank tower near Sunset and Vine. The Pacific Federal Building [1959], at 6801 Hollywood Boulevard, was one of the first new high-rise office buildings to go up on Hollywood Boulevard in twenty-five years. The spurt in office growth prompted Holiday Inn to build its high-rise motel on Highland Avenue in 1965. The high-rise boom that began in 1959 also brought a number of new structures to the Sunset Strip.

The new development attracted many new corporate tenants to Hollywood, and it brought in a multitude of smaller office-run businesses [such as travel agencies and import/exporters] and professionals [doctors, dentists, psychologists]. It was especially successful in bringing entertainment-related businesses [recording companies, television producers, music publishers, radio stations, and a host of lawyers, agents, and managers] to Hollywood—businesses that considered a Hollywood address on the letterhead eminently appropriate. The Sixties also saw the construction of the community's first new movie theater in decades: the Cinerama Dome, designed by innovative architect Welton Becket, and completed in 1963.

Developer Kaplan boasts that the new high-rise not only brought in business, but were also responsible for "cleaning up a lot of decrepit, honky-tonk type properties." Others take exception to this viewpoint, saying that regardless of the quality of the businesses housed in the older buildings, many of the structures torn down to make way for the new development were unique and beautiful. They claim that the old buildings were, in fact, aesthetically superior to the rather faceless towers, and more representative of the eclectic, expressive architecture that helped shape Hollywood's image in the 1920s.

Whatever artistic judgments are passed on the new towers, however, the fact remains that they provided a much-needed boost to Hollywood's professional economy. And none too soon, for rival development proceeded to spring up throughout Los Angeles, in Westwood, in Beverly Hills, in the western portion of the downtown area, and especially in that corporate phoenix rising from the old Fox lot—Century City.

The character of Hollywood's residential neighborhoods was also urbanized by the tremendous upsurge in multiple-dwelling units. Rezoned after the war, a huge chunk of Hollywood that was traditionally single-family homes began to absorb many new apartment houses. By 1963, Hollywood had almost fifty percent more housing units than it had in 1944, and population had soared from a depressed 158,000 in 1953 to more than 187,000, the area's wartime peak.

But the new-housing spurt did not turn out quite as the community had hoped, either aesthetically or financially. Property owners knocked down old houses and built larger ones, but the new structures were seldom of the same quality as the former dwellings. "We had neighborhoods that were upper income, which began to go to cheap,

In true Hollywood storybook fashion, Capitol Records grew from a Sunset and Vine storefront to this impressive tower, which is the world's first circular office building. The lights on the spire are traditional for the holiday season; photo 1960.

schlocky apartments," says Denver Miller, historic survey coordinator for the Hollywood Revitalization Committee. "The city didn't have a great deal of control out here. When they said, 'We'll make it all tall apartments,' they didn't attract the same cross-section." The area began to attract more elderly, more minorities, and more short-term residents. The number of single-family residences within the boundaries of Hollywood remained fairly constant, but that was due largely to the increased construction of expensive homes in the Hollywood hills. South of Franklin Avenue, Hollywood began to evolve into a district of people on their way up or on their way down.

In the mid-Sixties, Hollywood as a community absorbed another body blow—below the belt, so to speak—with the appearance and proliferation of "adult" movie theaters. A series of court decisions concerning obscenity laws, handed down around the time of the Free Speech Movement, decreased restrictions on what could be shown in a movie theater, and pornographic films went public in Hollywood—mostly because Hollywood had the

Bargain stores proliferated on Hollywood Boulevard like weeds when quality stores vacated during Hollywood's interregnum. This photo was taken in 1960, and it would be another fifteen years before a spirit of revitalization would take effect. Below: The Hollywood Market, at Hollywood and Whitley, was one of the last grocery stores on Hollywood Blvd.; photograph, 1960.

highest concentration of public screens.

The liberalization of motion picture exhibition standards had several negative effects on the area, not the least of which was the destruction of an important segment of Los Angeles' film culture —the art house movement, which film archivist and community activist Philip Chamberlin describes as having been "thriving" and vigorous" during the Fifties. "All the theaters that are now showing pornographic films were showing foreign-language films. The Vista, now a gay theater, specialized in Russian films...the [now] Pussycat on Santa Monica Boulevard ran Robert Bresson's *Diary of a Country Priest....*" The greater profitability of porno films left culture by the wayside; only Max Laemmle's Los Feliz Theater continued as an

art-film center in Hollywood.

Chamberlin, who remembers *The Immoral Mr. Teas* as the first film run publicly in Hollywood, where one could see a female breast on the screen, says that after the court decisions, "The town went berserk. Gradually it got so pornography was on a spree." Most of the questionable films shown during the mid-Sixties were "soft-core" films that would only garner an R-rating today, but it didn't take long for the traffic to bear increasingly explicit films.

Nor was it long before the rest of "adult" culture appeared in Hollywood. Pornographic book-shops, topless bars, massage parlors, and live sex shows infested "downtown" Hollywood and began to line Western Avenue and Santa Monica Boulevard. Crowds of street prostitutes began to do business along Sunset. By the late Sixties, the businesses of sex were firmly entrenched, severely straining the fabric of the community.

Many Hollywood residents and businessmen consider the rise of porn-related business the great-est single perpetrator of street crime and image

Above: What might have been: the architect's rendering of the Hollywood Museum, including a proposed glassed-in sound stage so that visitors could watch some of the moviemakers in action. It seemed that the museum's time had come. Land was acquired and many people inside and outside the entertainment industry actively supported the idea, but in the end, the high cost, city and movie-industry politics, petty jealousies, and big egos were a stumbling block, and the plan never came to fruition.

problems in Hollywood. The hustlers, themselves a problem, were an easy target for muggers and other attackers, and so were their customers. [The correlation between adult businesses and overt prostitution becomes especially strong with the idea that prostitution in Hollywood was not con-sidered an especially serious problem until the mid-Sixties, although Hollywood has always been an extremely high-traffic area.] Hollywood developed a newly unsavory street image, and lived down to it with increasing incidence of both "victimless" and violent crime.

The rock scene, the protest era, the hippies—the mid-Sixties cult and culture of youth—burst upon Hollywood with the intensity and color of a thousand movie premieres. Hollywood, along with other urban centers, became thronged with kids sporting the new look, new sound, and new values of hip American youth. Perceptions and opinions of the young people ranged from admiration to contempt; "generation gap" became a catch-phrase for the decade. No matter what one thought of the Sixties youth culture, however, one thing was clear, and remains so today: the kids had the power to transform the areas they flowed into, and their impact had proven to be lasting in cities around the country. Los Angeles is no exception, and Hollywood is where that impact was felt the most.

The first wave of the postwar baby boom reached adolescence as the Sixties got underway. Suddenly teenagers, by sheer weight of numbers, became an American presence to be reckoned with. Unlike most of their counterparts of the Fifties, these kids had great curiosity and a certain restlessness. They also had purchasing power. The cities and towns of America responded with an unprecedented number of activities and diversions geared toward the young people.

The lavish, expensive night clubs that had splashed the Sunset Strip with neon and glamour were gone by 1960, victims of the waning picture business and the exodus of nightclub entertainers to Las Vegas. After the buildings stood vacant for a few years, a few young entrepreneurs opened smaller, less expensive clubs and coffeehouses catering to the eighteen-to-thirty crowds. Even high schoolers were able to hang out at the clubs; the owners, helped by the strip's location in an unincorporated section of Los Angeles County, were able to obtain "youth permits," officially allowing them to admit minors as long as they were not served liquor.

The first few clubs caught on, and more appeared. The spirit-liberating thump of the new music resounded up and down the street from The Trip, The Daisy, Whisky-a-Go-Go, Pandora's Box, Gazzarri's, The Fifth Estate, and several others. The clean-cut Fifties look gave way to long hair, strange costumes, and stranger slogans. The streets and sidewalks became clogged with surfers, Ph.D. candidates, Hell's Angels, and high school sopho-

mores, all looking for a good time. And the tension began to mount.

Admittedly, the presence of so many unconventional youths did not do much to enhance the formerly glamorous strip's image during the first few years of the rock era. The kids moved into houses and apartments above Sunset Boulevard and turned them into crash pads. There was increasing experimentation with drugs, especially marijuana and amphetamines [diet pills—the strip's official high—were readily available from Mom's medicine chest and from street sources]. The sexual revolution, to the chagrin of many adults, had taken off in earnest.

Added to this was the fact that although many of the teenagers making the scene were local kids from nearby comfortable homes, a great number were out on the street without money, food, or a place to sleep. Drawn by Hollywood's glittering name, youths poured in from all over Southern California and the rest of the country looking for excitement. Some of them wound up in the shadow of the trendy shops at Sunset Plaza Drive, picking through the garbage behind Ben Frank's Coffee Shop. It wasn't a pretty sight.

But the worst problem, as far as adult residents of West Hollywood were concerned, was the traffic. The strip was, and is, a major thoroughfare between Hollywood and Beverly Hills, and locals did not appreciate the main drag becoming impassable with a convention of anarchists in pressed hair and bell bottoms.

When residents complained, the sheriff's department responded by invoking the old 10:00 P.M. curfew and carting off the under-eighteen crowd by the busload [sometimes entering coffeehouses and examining IDs], although the curfew was enforced nowhere else in the county. Nor did the police hesitate to use physical methods of persuasion on recalcitrant youngsters. Nor, once the kids had been taken in, were they quick to notify parents that their children had been arrested.

Not content to round up the juveniles, police used other methods of petty harassment, such as invoking an ordinance stating that musicians in clubs were not permitted to mingle with patrons and using it against young musicians who would stroll from table to table. They created a confrontation situation in 1966, when they interpreted a vague loitering law to define a loiterer as anyone who stopped moving on the street for more than a few seconds.

Pandora's Box, at the corner of Sunset and Crescent Heights, became the focal point of the conflict as the tension reached its height. The coffeehouse sat on a small island between the city limits and the area administered by the county. Sheriff's deputies would push crowds toward Pandora's Box from the west, while LAPD officers, not wishing a mass invasion of kids into Hollywood, drove them onto the triangle of land from the east. Once the kids were herded together, many were arrested for loitering or unlawful assembly.

By 1967, the youth scene had moved east to Hollywood proper. Young people congregated by the thousands at "love-ins" in Griffith and Elysian parks; psychedelic light shows and rock concerts were presented throughout the area. Many new Hollywood residents took part in the massive anti-war protest that demonstrated outside the Century Plaza Hotel during President Johnson's June 1967 Democratic fund-raiser. Each week, more and more kids left home or school or jobs and came to where the action was.

San Francisco was the cultural and ideological center at the beginning of the rock era, but when the dust settled on the Summer of Love, Los Angeles emerged as the most important locus of the hippie movement. It was bigger, more diverse, and more active politically. And even more importantly, it had Hollywood.

Hollywood Boulevard began to sprout businesses catering to the youth trade—record stores, book exchanges, and "head" shops carrying the paraphernalia of a turned-on society. Black lights replaced flourescent bulbs; love beads replaced fine jewelry. Hippies crowded into rented homes and hung posters proclaiming an era of peace and love at hand. The invasion was swift and thorough.

The area was polarized immediately between the high-living kids on the one hand and the "Establishment"—the long-time residents, businessmen, property owners, politicians, and police—on the other. They gave full-throated cry against the invaders. They were turning houses into rubble, the old-timers screamed; they were filling the air with marijuana; they were bringing crime to unprecedented levels; they were ruining the image of Hollywood.

It isn't difficult to understand why the old-timers were threatened and upset. For years, Hollywood had been a family neighborhood, and now it was overrun by kids who looked like nobody's children—unkempt, freaked-out, and heedless of authority. They were an eyesore and a nuisance.

And crime did go up—everything from panhandling to vandalism. Drug deals were conducted on the street; young girls and boys joined the ranks of the prostitutes. Frustrated by what they saw as an unfeeling, violent society, sometimes hungry and homeless, the young people often handled things badly.

"You've got to figure that if you have people who don't have enough money and are living on the streets, a certain amount of crime is going to happen," says film publicist Charles Lippincott, a producer of light shows and a frequent visitor to Hollywood during and after his student days at USC. "But with reporting crime it depends on how the police feel at the time—whom they want to pick up, and whom they don't want to pick up. Their activity was aimed at young people—a rebellious group that represented the Vietnam War situation, the drug situation, the music that they didn't like...." For their part, the hippies made the police "more of a target than they are now" because "they represented the repression."

It is also true that communes and other living arrangements made by the youngsters made a shambles out of many residences, but the door had been opened for them long before, when Hollywood's property owners turned their backs on the area and became absentee landlords.

The business district of Hollywood and the residential area around it was gaudy, noisy, and

THESE PROPERTIES BEING ACQUIRED

FOR THE SITE OF
——— THE ———
LOS ANGELES COUNTY HOLLYWOOD MUSEUM

MOTION PICTURES. TELEVISION. RADIO & RECORDING

Dedication ceremonies at the Hollywood Museum site; 1961.

replete with rejection of the old guard's values by 1967, and it remained so for the rest of the decade. Many established Hollywoodites resented their hometown being turned into a twenty-four-hour carnival, and still blame the youth movement for the continuing decay of the area.

But other long-time residents defended the youths for bringing new color and life to what had been becoming a rather nondescript cityscape. "Overall, I think it had a good effect," Charles Lippincott muses. "I don't think Hollywood had any personality of its own [at the time]…it was losing any it had." The street life on the boulevard has never had more vitality."

There's no doubt that the years of youth protest were painful ones for Hollywood. They were the years before the enlightened populism of the Seventies; the younger and older generations seemed to be on opposite sides of almost every issue. It was an equally scary time for those seeking

radical change and those trying to hold on to the status quo. The late Sixties were a period of confrontation in an area that had avoided confronting its problems for a long time.

On the local media front, the key word was "underground." Underground films were run at the strip's Cinematheque 16; underground video, music, and theater was created and patronized by the artistically hip.

The word underground is used the most, though, in describing the alternative newspapers that were published by and for the counterculture. Several of these appeared in Los Angeles, but the two most influential were *Open City*, founded and copublished by Bob Garcia, now a top executive with A & M Records, and the longer-lived L.A. *Free Press*, founded in 1964 by Art Kunkin. Each served as a forum for the counterculture community and covered events that were of little interest to regional dailies.

During the Sixties, the film industry failed to gain much momentum quantitatively or qualitatively. A slight rise in revenues in 1965 was due mainly to the huge success of a few big-budget films [*Goldfinger, My Fair Lady, The Sound of Music, Dr. Zhivago*] that set the tone for major releases—though not for their success—in years to come. In a 1967 *Look* magazine column, William Zinsser bemoaned the creative malaise in Hollywood: "The old excitement has died, and some of the preeminence. It is hard not to feel a sharp burst of apathy, for instance, at the thought of the big studios still making safe "blockbusters" like *Hello, Dolly!* when filmmakers everywhere else—especially in New York and Europe—are doing work that is experimental and offbeat." The majors, of course, continued their policy of big, "safe" pictures through the rest of the decade and into the Seventies. But the policy backfired; most of the expensive productions lost money, and the early Seventies marked a nadir in the creative and financial fortunes of the film industry.

Geographically, one of the movies' power centers had moved over the hill to Universal, which loomed as even more of a behemoth after its purchase by entertainment conglomerate MCA, Inc. MCA, which had formerly functioned as a mammoth talent agency, swallowed up record companies, book publishers, television shows, and film producers, and dominated the entertainment industry from its black tower in Universal City.

When Columbia Pictures vacated its Sunset-Gower facility and moved on the lot with Warner Brothers at the Burbank studios in 1972, the only major film company left in Hollywood was Paramount Pictures.

By the late Sixties, the local film industry was also plagued with increasing numbers of "runaway" productions—pictures financed by major studios but shot outside of Los Angeles for tax benefits, foreign subsidies, and other financial reasons: "It's cheaper," one producer told the *Los Angeles Times* in 1968. "I can go to Yugoslavia and get the whole damn army for one-dollar a day and

lunch." Producers shooting abroad could dispense with the problems and expense of Los Angeles guilds and technical unions. Other American locations, especially New York, cut the red tape of filmmaking to bring film company dollars to their towns. Unemployment among Los Angeles film personnel soared.

But the movies were not the only game in town, and the rest of the entertainment industry came to Hollywood with the rush of the Seventh Cavalry. The recording industry, stepchild of the music business since its development, burst into its own with the advent of rock music. Whatever the old-timers thought of rock's aesthetics and social content, it had the power to bring jobs, talent, and dollars to Hollywood.

The area had enjoyed an active youth-oriented live music scene even before the rock era broke. Folk clubs such as Cosmo Alley and the Ashgrove [now the Improvisation] drew crowds; Soul'd Out, still open on Sunset Boulevard, was a haven for twisters in the early Sixties. Los Angeles, along with other cities, kept a close eye on the nation's spawning grounds for new music, such as the Newport Jazz Festival. When the Beatles came to the Colonies and rock plugged itself in, the Hollywood cultural scene became as electrified as Bob Dylan's guitar.

Led by the seminal Byrds, Los Angeles-based groups became an important factor on the national rock scene. Canned Heat, the Velvet Underground, Johnny Rivers, the Mamas and the Papas, the Standells, Tim Hardin, Frank Zappa, and the Doors were among the hot new performers that developed and worked in Los Angeles. The Sunset Strip was a live-performance center for the entire Southwest. Super-producer Phil Spector [a Fairfax High alumnus] and the now-Lieutenant Governor Mike Curb opened offices and studios here and helped start the trend that eventually moved the center of the recording industry from New York to Los Angeles.

The record business, which had never pushed the sale of long-playing albums before, developed sophisticated new marketing techniques to exploit

Above: Looking south on Vine Street from
Franklin Avenue during the holiday
season, 1964. At left: The dining room
of the Vine Street Derby, 1961.
The building was built by Cecil B.
DeMille, but Herbert Samborn
founded the Brown Derby and opened it
on Valentine's Day, 1929. Still the
dining place of celebrities, the
Derby is best known for its caricatures
of movie and recording stars and
for its Cobb Salad, named for its
former owners, Bob and Sally Cobb.

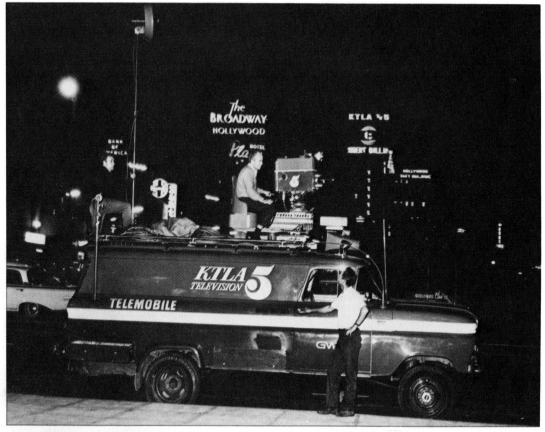

Above: KTLA's mobile truck, parked near Selma and Vine, 1965, is a sophisticated contrast to its W6XYZ experimental rig of eighteen years earlier. At left: The Cinerama Dome Theater, on Sunset, west of Vine, is one of the first theaters in the world built exclusively for cinerama. Opposite page: An aerial view of downtown Hollywood; the street running up the center is Hollywood Boulevard; the cross street near the bottom of the photo is La Brea.

them. They told the students of America that if you loved your rock stars, you'd buy their LPs, and the youth of America obeyed.

David W. Lawhon, president of manufacturing for Capitol Records, and Robert Karp, the company's chief legal counsel, explain the evolution of Hollywood as the recording capital. "The recording business was not a very affluent business until the Sixties—until rock hit the scene. Most [older] artists did not make a living from making phonograph records...the record business was sort of a sideline," says Karp. But with the appearance of performers who did make most of their living as recording artists, the record companies wanted to be where their stars were.

Many musicians and their managers were already in Southern California; others settled out here because, as Lawhon describes it, "a high percentage of affluent people who can choose where they want to live choose Southern California." He explains that "the recording industry survives on

its artists and its music, not on its factories and distribution systems, and they need to be where their talent is."

Once the decision to move to California was made, there was a "natural gravitation" to the Hollywood area, "since Hollywood had a name that was associated with entertainment." Hollywood had new office space and was building more, both in Hollywood proper and along the Sunset Strip. Support services were excellent; Los Angeles had the best concentration of studio musicians and production engineers, and a wealth of legal talent to serve the record community. Recording studios sprang up throughout the area because, according to Lawhon, "the words 'Hollywood' and 'studio' are sort of synonymous."

The fact that few major recording companies, most notably Capitol, were Hollywood fixtures long before 1964 helped spur the recording boom in the area. Herb Alpert and Jerry Moss founded instant-success A & M Records, which moved into

and restored the old Charlie Chaplin Studios at Sunset and La Brea in 1966. An accelerating migration from New York, Nashville, Chicago, and Detroit rolled in as the Sixties progressed; once a good chunk of the industry had come to Los Angeles, most of the others followed. And as the record companies gained in power, many of them began to diversify into entertainment fields that necessitated a move to Los Angeles. Multimillion dollar Motown Records, which in less than ten years had made Stevie Wonder, Diana Ross, the Temptations, the Jackson 5, Marvin Gaye, and Gladys Knight household sounds, moved from Detroit to Hollywood in 1970, joining such popular labels as Liberty [later United Artists], Polydor, and Elektra.

As the Seventies opened, the music of the street people had translated into plush corporate offices up and down Sunset Boulevard.

Progress among the other performing arts was equally heartening. Los Angeles had already been established as a television production center, overtaking New York during the Fifties, and it continued to strengthen its position. Hollywood was the locale for two of the three network facilities after KNBC moved to Burbank in 1963; the four

major local stations [KTLA, KHJ, KTTV, and KCOP] remained, and several UHF stations [including KCET, a number of Spanish-language outlets, and KWHY, the first television station in America to broadcast a full daily program of financial news] helped make Hollywood a local broadcast center. Television programmers depended increasingly on Hollywood facilities and offices, including the Vine Street Theatre, the TAV celebrity Theater, and the Hollywood Palace; many live shows of the Sixties emanated from Hollywood. "Shindig," Los Angeles' 1965 answer to "American Bandstand," came out of KABC's studios on Prospect Avenue. And by the end of the decade, Los Angeles was also home to many talk shows.

Radio stations were also established in Hollywood studios. The CBS facility at Sunset and Gower housed KNXT-AM [which switched from pop music to an all-news format in 1968] and KNX-FM, a soft-rock station, which was established in 1966. KPOL, at 5700 Sunset, combined easy-listening music with extensive news and community-affairs coverage. Public Radio KPFK moved from Melrose and Larchmont to Cahuenga in 1961 and

Dino's Lodge, on the Sunset Strip, was the location for the hit television series *77 Sunset Strip* and a popular supper club. It's under new ownership today, and it is now called Chez Denis.

continued its eclectic programming, including controversial political coverage. Station KMET, founded at 5746 Sunset in 1961, led the way for other Hollywood-based FM rock stations, a trend that was to accelerate during the Seventies.

On the live-theater scene, the Huntington Hartford continued going strong. Theatergoers from suburbs throughout the basin were drawn by such plays as *The Tenth Man, The Subject Was Roses, The Homecoming,* and *Under Milkwood.* Little theater flourished as well. Many small companies that were created during the arts-nurturing mid-Sixties are still active in presenting new or hitherto seldom-produced stage works; among the more active theaters are The Melrose Theatre, the New Playwright's Foundation, Actors Studio West, Theatre Rapport, The Hyperion Theatre, East/West Players, and The Evergreen Stage Company.

For the young actor, director, musician, technician, producer, and writer, Hollywood remained what it had always been: Mecca.

Statistics do not show the emotional and sociological changes Hollywood went through during the Sixties. The population remained predominantly Anglo, though not as overwhelmingly; by 1970, about one out of six persons was a Latino, and Orientals—especially Koreans and Thais—were beginning to shore up the business district between Vine and Vermont. The under-thirty group had grown from thirty to thirty-seven percent of the total, but they were equalled in number by the middle-aged group. The renter population, which was enormous in 1960, got a little more enormous. The statistics relate information about households containing unrelated persons, but they do not show the invasion of the hippies. They chronicle changes in per capita income, but they do not count up the ravages of absentee landlords.

By the end of the decade, Hollywood's population had grown to 214,000, and city planners were projecting that more than 350,000 people would live there in twenty years. In June of 1969, three concepts for Hollywood's future growth were presented to its citizens. One of them envisioned Hollywood as a sprawling, low-rise residential and business community, held together by a new Los Angeles rapid-transit network. Another would have created an even more suburban atmosphere, complete with parks and a wide range of housing types; this plan was dependent on construction of the Beverly Hills Freeway, proposed during the Sixties. The plan that seems to have taken hold the most was one that called for Hollywood's continued development as an urban center with more high-rise office and residential buildings and improved shopping and tourist attractions—the "urbanization" that had begun during the early Sixties. It must have seemed amazing to many Hollywood residents that plans for the development of Hollywood were still being announced, after all the plans and promises that had failed.

But the amazing thing about Hollywood in the Sixties is that it held up as well as it did. If the picture industry slowed to a crawl, it still did not diminish Hollywood's preeminence as a place to see movies [Westwood, where many of the movie houses have only opened in the last ten years, did not become a real threat until the Seventies] and did not remove the industry support services—labs, equipment rentals, agencies, and law firms—that have contributed so much to the area. Newer entertainment businesses filled the void left by departing film companies and have flourished in the nurturing climate.

If the hippies helped put the finish to Hollywood as a middle-class bedroom and retail community, there are those who argue that they didn't do anything that wouldn't have happened without them. And when the fever of the youth movement broke and the disillusioned left, they left behind a group of young activists who looked around and saw a community in big trouble—and decided to do something about it. Nor could the avarice and apathy that sped the area's deterioration deter the dedicated old guard—the Kiwanis men, the Rotarians, and other service clubs—from trying to save the town they love.

Hollywood has always been exported, in films, television programs, and recordings. As a result, Hollywood has been called the magnet that draws businesses to Southern California. If certain companies turn up their noses at Hollywood and settle elsewhere in the basin, it is probably be-

cause the magic name "Hollywood" that attracted them to become part of the Southern California economy had lost its allure.

The Hollywood Museum

One of the most publicized and glamorous projects in Los Angeles' history was the controversial Hollywood Museum. During the six-year planning period, the proposed museum gained the backing of top entertainers, producers, directors, influential business executives, and high-ranking political leaders. However, in spite of all this elite, high-powered community support, the Hollywood Museum was destined to failure even before one shovelful of dirt was turned.

The concept for a motion picture museum had been the subject of discussion for many years in Hollywood, but it wasn't until noted film executive Sol Lesser became involved that things began to happen. Lesser approached County Supervisor Ernest E. Debs and the Hollywood Chamber of Commerce with his idea for a museum, which would pay tribute to the business that made Hollywood famous. Within a few short weeks, word of the proposed plan sparked immediate enthusiasm in the community, especially among those in the entertainment industry.

The first step in the creation of the museum occurred on June 16, 1959, when the Hollywood Motion Picture and Television Museum Commission was created by an ordinance of the County Board of Supervisors.

The board established an eleven-member commission charged with the responsibility "to foster and perpetuate interest in the history of the motion picture and television industries by construction, operation, and maintenance of a museum in the Hollywood area." Sol Lesser was unanimously elected to head the commission, which included representatives of the major motion picture guilds and studios, television companies, and the Hollywood Chamber of Commerce.

The second step in the development of the

M'Goo's, on the corner of Hollywood Boulevard and Cherokee, was a favorite 60's hangout before it burned down; photo, 1969.

museum was the commissioning of the architectural firm of William L. Pereira and Associates to design and prepare plans and specifications for the institution. In June 1960, at a rally of top film and TV stars and executives at the Screen Directors Guild Theater, Pereira presented preliminary sketches and plans for the much-talked-about Hollywood Museum. The proposed rectangular structure was to have a total floor space of 120,000 square feet [excluding two sound stages and their supporting areas]. Of this total, about 96,000 square feet were to be allocated to active museum space with the remaining 24,000 square feet devoted to such service functions as stairs, receiving and preparation areas, and rest rooms. Of the 96,000 square feet within the museum's active area, 2,200 were to be devoted to a conventional library and another 5,500 for an electronic library. The remaining space was to be allocated to dis-

plays, exhibits, theaters, and similar activities. Because of the preliminary plans being received with such overwhelming response, William Pereira was given the go-ahead to complete final plans and specifications for the museum.

At the same time that the preliminary plans were unveiled, Sol Lesser announced the formation of the Hollywood Museum Associates, Inc., which was to function as the artifact and fund-raising arm of the museum. With such distinguished members as Lucille Ball, Cecilia DeMille, Mrs. L.B. Mayer, Mrs. Leiland Atherton Irish, and C.E. Toberman, the associates began a vigorous campaign to raise several million dollars in industrial exhibit sponsorships as well as private and personal gifts. In addition, the group began to solicit contributions of old films, historical printed material, and all types of movie memorabelia and artifacts that would be displayed and used in the proposed museum.

With tentative plans drawn, and several committees actively working, the commission began looking at various sites for the museum. After considering many possible locations, it was finally decided that the ideal site would be on the east side of Highland Avenue, just south of the main entrance of the Hollywood Bowl. The selection of this location would also give additional, desperately needed, parking to the Hollywood Bowl.

Shortly after the County Board of Supervisors placed its stamp of approval on the museum site, condemnation proceedings began, followed by the demolition of the old structures. It was at this point that the museum got its first dose of adverse publicity, when Steven Anthony, one of the owners of the condemned property, refused to sell his home to the county. For months, Anthony delayed the progress of the museum by exhausting every legal remedy at his disposal. When the case was eventually heard in court, the jury awarded Anthony $11,750 for his property. Anthony appealed and the appellate court upheld the lower court's decision. Finally, when both the California and U.S. Supreme Courts refused to intervene, Anthony stood off eviction with a loaded shotgun for a period of ten weeks. Tricked, seized, and booked for "obstructing a police officer in the performance of his duty," he bailed out only to find workmen knocking his home to splinters.

By early 1964, the formation and development of the Hollywood Museum seemed to be in full swing. Plans were being finalized, funds raised, artifacts and historical material donated, curators and staff members appointed, and, of course, land was being acquired. However, when the final plans and specifications were carefully analyzed, it became clear to many people that the museum would not be financially self-sufficient, as originally intended. Based on a projected cost of $21 million, as well as the intricate and complex nature of the recommended facility, it appeared that from $4 to $6 million would be required annually for operation, maintenance, and debt service.

It wasn't long until the Hollywood Museum began to experience some rough going. With staunch proponents on one side and critics on the other, the five-year-old project soon became one of the city's most controversial issues of the decade.

In order to provide an impartial review of the financial soundness of the project and an appraisal of its future, the County Board of Supervisors appointed the Hollywood Cultural Center Study Committee in November 1964. Committee members were Bart Lytton, President and Board Chairman, Lytton Financial; Dr. Franklin D. Murphy, Chancellor, University of California at Los Angeles; and Harrison A. Price, President, Economics Research Company. As the newly appointed committee began its analytical review of the project, the County Board of Supervisors called for a complete "freeze" on further development of the museum pending final report from the three-man committee. Up to this point, the county had invested $1,122,504 for architectural plans, operating expenses, and acquisitions of the site opposite the Hollywood Bowl.

Six months after its formation, the committee filed its final report confirming the fact that, under the present financial and organizational structure, the proposed museum would require substantial subsidy for many years. However, the study did acknowledge that the museum had great potential if major alterations were made in the proposed structure, operating plans, and financing.

By this time, the County Board of Supervisors realized they had a political "hot potato" on their hands, and they wanted to get rid of it. Therefore, in October of 1965, the county withdrew its support of the project, thereby forcing the commission to curtail administrative operations. The many artifacts, films, and historical material, which had been donated by the countless supporters, were turned over to the Department of Parks and Recreation for safekeeping.

The abandonment of the Hollywood Museum project marked the end of a six-year struggle for what would have been the finest testimony to one of the world's most glamorous industries—the motion picture business.

Part Five:
1970-1979

The 1960s and early 1970s were periods of decline the likes of which Hollywood hadn't seen since the Crash of '29. Although the city's profile had begun to take on a shiny, high-rise look, it was crumbling within—an implosion that seemed at first irreversible. Office buildings—including the new ones—were only fifty-to-sixty-percent occupied, at best. Small specialty shops were deserting to more prestigious locations like Beverly Hills and Westwood; major department store chains, though building elsewhere at an accelerated rate, weren't interested in taking a chance on the city, a problem that Los Angeles city planner Frank Fielding, who had put together the 1970 development concept, attributed to "a lack of faith in Hollywood." And, indeed, in the early dawn of the Seventies, faith wasn't the city's strong suit.

The lack of community support for its newspaper was symptomatic of Hollywood's malaise. The *Citizen News* had been in the hands of the Palmer family for more than forty years when its publisher, Harlan Palmer, Jr., sold the popular newspaper to David B. Heyler, Sr. on December 29, 1961. Heyler, who was also the owner of the *Beverly Hills Citizen*, published the Hollywood-based *Citizen News* until 1966, when he, in turn, sold it to Lammont du Pont Copeland. Within a couple of years, financial difficulties began to plague the newspaper, and by March 1970, the problem was critical. Copeland reorganized the paper's corporate structure under Graphic Productions, Inc., and at the same time, changed the newspaper's name to *Los Angeles Evening Citizen News*. However, this maneuver proved to be an exercise in futility, for in August 1970, the Internal Revenue Service seized the assets of the newspaper. It was allowed to continue operation for an additional two weeks, at which time it was realized that the financial ills were incurable. Much to the disappointment of the

citizens of Hollywood, the last issue of the famed, sixty-six-year-old newspaper was published on Friday, August 28, 1970.

An economic depression in the film industry hit Hollywood hard in 1971. Some studios shut down; a major [Columbia] relocated, and its sound stages were converted to tennis courts; nearly all of them had critically curtailed production. Television, which had propped up the toppling movie industry during the Fifties and Sixties, was shooting fewer and fewer programs here. By March of 1971, fifty percent of the local film-union members were out of work. Lines grew ominously long at the state department of employment office, a squatty brick building on Santa Monica Boulevard that, up to then, had gone largely unnoticed by passersby. Unemployment has always been seasonal and more sporadic in the entertainment industry than in other trades and professions, but never in the numbers that were lining up in front of the employment office in 1971.

Movie industry leaders were calling it "Hollywood's worst depression," and many of them wondered aloud—in the press—whether it could be turned around. Jack Foreman, chief executive at Samuel Goldwyn Studios and former president of the Hollywood Chamber of Commerce, recalled, "Deterioration was setting in so fast—even geographically—that it shook everybody up. Something had to be done."

Indeed, something had to be done, Hollywood's malady was more than economic; it was sociological as well. At the feet of the shiny high-rises along Sunset and Hollywood boulevards lay what was beginning to be called Sin City, in which pornography was the heir apparent. Festering pockets of sexbook stores, sex shops, strip joints, clip joints, sex-movie houses, massage parlors, and the like were catering to a new clientele of drifting dregs from the flower-child Sixties, dopers, dealers, drag queens, pimps, prostitutes, muggers, transients, crazies, and other unsavory sorts, who were drawn to the area like maggots to rotting flesh. They changed Hollywood's physical image in the extreme. And the irony is that most of them were probably drawn to Hollywood owing to its pre-Sixties image, the clean, glossy, glamorous Thirties and Forties image that still lives on large and small screens throughout the world.

In no group was Hollywood's geographically wide magnetic attraction more evident than the prostitutes, who descended on the city like locusts. According to Captain Jerry Feinberg of the Los Angeles Police Department's Hollywood Division, the prostitutes zeroed in on Hollywood from as far away as Miami and Detroit. They came, according to Captain Feinberg, "because they heard that business was so lucrative." And they came in such numbers that one could rarely stroll along Sunset Boulevard or the Western Avenue area [the places where they congregated in the greatest numbers] without being propositioned.

As prostitutes were attracted to Hollywood, so, too, were other unsavory elements. Angry citizens called for more and better police protection, but the solution wasn't that easy. Hollywood's a relatively small town, but owing to its attraction for others, it has big-city problems. From 1969 through 1975, Hollywood's crime rate increased 7.6 percent—nearly double that of Los Angeles' city-wide crime-rate increase during the same period. No city of comparable size in the nation has quite the problem that Hollywood police are saddled with. And it's doubtful that any city had less community support.

On the economic front, the only bright spot in the early Seventies was the recording business and its supportive crafts, which had come to town in large numbers with the advent of rock music in the 1960s. The popularity of rock also boosted local radio, particularly the FM stations, which had been largely an esoteric medium until the Seventies.

Another ray of light burst forth on September 25, 1973, when the Los Angeles City Planning Commission adopted a new master plan for Hollywood, one designed to make the city a better place

Just your average Sunday morning on Hollywood Boulevard. Well, not exactly average, but not that unusual, either. An MGM crew shooting a scene for the film *Alex in Wonderland*, 1970. Location shooting is almost a daily occurrence in Hollywood.

to work, live, and visit. Characteristically, the plan had been three years in the making, and it had taken another three years of disputes and haggling in the Los Angeles City Council before it was approved. But devising and approving a plan is one thing; carrying it out is quite another.

The Task Force

After the death of her husband, Robert, Peggy Stevenson ran for his council seat and won. She took office as the representative of the 13th District, which includes the communities of Hollywood, Highland Park, Hollywood Hills, Los Feliz, and Silverlake, among others.

Councilwoman Stevenson is a native of Hollywood and a graduate of Fairfax High School and UCLA; she knows her district well. "Hollywood's problems are the result of thirty-five years of public and private neglect," she said. "It's going to take the full resources of government and the community to undo those years."

One of Peggy Stevenson's first actions was to establish the Revitalize Hollywood Task Force in 1975, calling for the turnaround of the city as the task force's first priority. She met with resistance in convincing other city officials of the importance of Hollywood's revitalization, but she finally received the support of Mayor Tom Bradley and federal officials.

This is not to say that Hollywood was at a complete standstill until the revitalization plan began taking shape, but that the building and restoring that was being done was not a concerted effort. There was very little collective development planning.

"All the effort that was taking place was fragmented then," said Mann Theaters' William Hertz, the 1979 Chamber of Commerce president. "It was a real problem. People were going off in their own diverse directions. But now, since we put together the sign, everyone is thinking togetherness. The prognosis of bringing Hollywood to what it really should be is unlimited."

Among the individual-effort improvements to the city's appearance made during 1976 were the Gower Gulch specialty shopping center, the remodeling of Sunset Gower Independent Studios [the former home of Columbia Pictures], a new Cooper's Home Improvement Center on Sunset and Western, the $750,000 remodeling of an old Sunset Boulevard building by the Old Spaghetti Factory restaurant, and A&M Records' modern accounting building, located on La Brea, just south of the historic Charlie Chaplin Studios, which A&M Records occupies and which has been kept in excellent repair.

By July 1976, the Revitalize Hollywood Task Force of thirty-four citizens made public its report. It began: "Hollywood is at a crossroads." Accurate, surely, and about the kindest way to say it. The ambitious study called for construction of park malls and a central plaza in the business area, development of shopping center complexes in the Hollywood core, refurbishing of business fronts along Hollywood Boulevard and nearby streets, landscaping, and possible new transit systems within the city.

The committee suggested that the many-faceted program could be financed through federal grants, tax incentives for businesses to expand, assessment districts, a nonprofit corporation, and city and private donor funding.

The report did not ignore the high-crime problems, the low state of real estate in Hollywood, particularly in its flatland areas, where housing stock is the oldest in the city of Los Angeles. It also dealt with the urban decay, caused, in part, by the high degree of absentee landlordism here.

And it was also recommended that Hollywood recognize the large gay community living and working within its environs and that steps be taken to lessen law enforcement hostility toward homosexuals.

A month after the committee issued its report, the Los Angeles City Council authorized the Community Redevelopment Agency to give the Revitalize Hollywood project $100,000 to get underway. It wasn't much, considering the great sums it would take to put Hollywood back on its feet, but

Above: In the spring of 1979, Hollywood saw the addition of two 750-seat movie theaters adjacent to the Chinese Theatre. The new complex now has 3,000 seats in three theaters, one of the largest of its kind in the world. Left to right: Chamber President William F. Hertz, Councilwoman Peggy Stevenson, Ted Mann, Rhonda Fleming (Mrs. Ted Mann) and Mayor Tom Bradley. Left: Superstar Burt Reynolds receives his star in the Walk of Fame with William F. Hertz, Chamber President, actor Dom Deluise, Jack Foreman, Past Chamber President, Bob Seitz, Chamber Membership Director and Monty Hall, Honorary Mayor of Hollywood.

it was a start. And things began to happen.

"The enthusiasm changed, so did the direction, and Hollywood's self-concept," says executive director of the Hollywood Chamber Mike Sims, who came to work here in 1975. "People stopped badmouthing themselves and got to work. They said 'We've got everything, and we ought to be able to do something with it.' Councilwoman Stevenson and the chamber decided to concentrate on how Los Angeles sees Hollywood. Our local image. We didn't have to worry much about what the rest of the world thinks. They still think of Hollywood as Hollywood, a magic place, or they wouldn't keep coming here in droves."

Early in 1977, Hollywood's historic Pantages Theater became the city's "newest" live theater

The home of Merv Griffin's popular syndicated talk show is the TAV Celebrity Theater, on the west side of Vine Street, between Selma Avenue and Sunset Boulevard. The Celebrity Theater was once the West Coast home of the ABC radio and television networks in radio's golden days. The huge NBC radio complex was across the street, on Sunset and Vine; CBS was—and still is—just east, on Sunset Boulevard. This photograph was taken in 1976.

Above: Wallichs Music city was the first record store to use the self-service concept; after nearly forty years at its northwest corner on Sunset and Vine, Wallichs closed its doors in 1978.

when James Nederlander, of Nederlander Productions—which operates the Greek Theatre—and William Forman of Pacific Theaters became partners in converting the famous theater for legitimate stage productions. It was a boon to the theater world of Los Angeles, as well as to Hollywood.

The Pantages, designed and built by B. Marcus Preteca in 1930 [he also built the Orpheum in San Francisco] as a movie house, is an irreplaceable city landmark.

The Broadway musical *Bubbling Brown Sugar* opened to the public on February 16, forty-seven years after the Pantages showed its first movie in 1930: Marion Davies, starring in *Floradora Girl*.

The transfer of the Pantages to the live-theater roles increased Hollywood's total number of seats for live entertainment to 36,000 which includes the large stages of the Bowl, the Greek, the Holly-

wood Amphitheater, the Aquarius, the Huntington Hartford, those of smaller-capacity houses, such as the Pilot and Virginia Spolin theaters.

As the commercial core of Hollywood began an about-face, so did the city's pornography businesses. Since the worst years of 1974, 1975, and 1976, much of the pornographic trade has diminished. And many of the Western Avenue area's sex shops, bookstores, and massage parlors closed, thanks, in great part, to a city ordinance finally passed by council in the summer of 1978, after a year's ado. The ordinance, modeled after one in Detroit, limits adult-entertainment businesses, preventing them from being established within 1,000 feet of each other and within 500 feet of churches or schools.

In mid-1979, the LAPDs Hollywood Division, one of Los Angeles' busiest commands, began a task force crackdown on prostitution in Hollywood. Although it wasn't the first of such efforts, it was one of the most successful. In three months, police had made more than 1,000 arrests.

Crime, however, particularly violent crime, is still on the rise in Hollywood [up fourteen-percent from 1970 to 1978], as it is across the country. But police officials are hoping to slow its increase here by limiting or discouraging prostitution.

"The bottom line," says Hollywood area commander Feinberg, "is that we have a street crime

problem. Most of it is related to prostitution, narcotics, runaways, and street robberies. We're concentrating on those activities."

Above: The Magic Castle, at Franklin Avenue and Orange Drive, was built as a residence by Rollin Lane in 1910 at a cost of $12,000. Today it operates as a private club for magicians and for those interested in magic; this photo taken in 1976.

The Hollywood Sign As Symbol

At the beginning of the economic and physical turnabout, though, residents, business people, and politicians began to look north from Hollywood Boulevard toward Mt. Lee, one of the brush-covered hillsides that separates the Los Angeles Basin from the San Fernando Valley. There the HOLLYWOOD sign stood in disrepair, like Humpty Dumpty, about to fall down.

The chamber's Mike Sims said it first. "If you can't save the sign, you can't save Hollywood." And the sign became, for many in Hollywood, a symbol of Hollywood's past image and its present deterioration. Age, rainstorms, and wind had taken their toll on the giant monument, and the HOLLYWOOD sign stood rotting and rusting on its mountainside.

The sign, which could be seen for twenty-five miles on a clear day, remained in good condition until 1964, when it began to show serious signs of weather damage. It continued to deteriorate until 1970, when the Hollywood Kiwanians adopted it as a project and restored it for $4,500.

In 1973, sign sentimentalists won out over those who wanted it torn down, and the Los Angeles Cultural Heritage Board declared it Historic Cultural Monument No. 111, thus giving it some prestige, but no funds for its repair.

The chamber directed another fund-raising campaign and hundreds of contributions came in, including a generous donation from Les Kelley, publisher of the Kelley Blue Book, who pledged $1,000 a year for ten years to maintain it.

A Hollywood-style extravaganza that year, complete with silent film star Gloria Swanson and kleig lights, was scheduled, but the occasion was

269

Left: In 1977, the Pantages went legit with the Broadway hit *Bubbling Brown Sugar.* Above: Herb Alpert's 1977 Walk of Fame ceremony. At Alpert's side are his mother, Tillie Alpert, and his wife, singer Lani Hall; also pictured from left to right are: Mike Sims, director of the chamber of commerce; actress Jane Withers; William Hertz, president of the chamber; Mayor of Los Angeles, Tom Bradley, and the Alpert's two daughters.

never seen by onlookers. A heavy fog rolled eastward that night down Sunset from the ocean and crept up the hills just as the ceremony began.

By early 1977, as rejuvenation for the city below it was coming into swing, the HOLLYWOOD sign was in bad shape again. This time, there had been so much structural damage that engineers who examined it said it probably ought to be torn down and rebuilt. The top of its D was gone, and officials feared the entire letter would topple soon. The Hollywood chamber used the last of its sign funds, $4,500, that spring to repair the damaged D.

Then the first O fell apart, the third one toppled down the mountain, and in November an arsonist set fire to the sign, burning the bottom portion of the second L.

The fight to save the landmark began with a "Save the Sign" campaign. It was an uphill battle for Mike Sims and the rest of the Hollywood Chamber, and at times it looked hopeless.

In June 1977, Sims thought they had come up with the fund-raising answer to get the $250,000 needed to demolish the old sign and rebuild a new one, but he was foiled again.

A popular rock group, Fleetwood Mac, agreed to do a charity concert at the Hollywood Bowl for the sign, but a few residents near the bowl, obviously not in a sign-saving mood, objected to having a rock band perform there using its own amplification system. They said it would be too loud. [The bowl's sound system is set for a maximum of ninety decibels.] No amount of pleading could

Above: The Hollywood sign was in shambles in this early 1978 photo. Right: It took a helicopter and daredevil workmen to assemble the steel braces that would eventually hold the huge letters in place; the cost of each of the letters was $27,700.

change their minds.

For almost a year, nothing happened. In April 1978, Grey Advertising donated an expensive multimedia campaign to do radio and TV spots. Another group sold "I Helped Hollywood" T-shirts, but money only dribbled in.

Playboy magazine publisher Hugh Hefner, who moved to Los Angeles a few years ago, opened up his mansion for a posh benefit for the sign, which netted about $45,000. Hefner picked up the tab for the food, drink, and entertainment for the $150-a-person party, and for this effort, the Y was dedicated in his name.

Hefner, who calls the sign "Hollywood's Eiffel Tower," would make more significant contributions to the city in 1979, among them the first Playboy Jazz Festival, patterned after the East Coast's Newport Jazz event, destined, "in all probability because of public and community accept-

ance," he said, to become an annual event.

"Hollywood is my new home," said Hefner, "and I expect to spend the rest of my life here, so I have a very real commitment to the revitalization of the community and to its interests."

In late June of '78, rock star Alice Cooper, long a Hollywood devotee, gave the next major contribution for the sign: $27,700, the price for reconstructing one of the letters. He said he wanted to buy the last O in memory of his friend, the late Groucho Marx. "After all this time," said smiling Mike Sims, "I just can't believe it."

On the whole, the donors of the new letters for the sign are a conglomeration of sorts, representing the diversity of the city, which is, as Mayor Bradley puts it, "a remarkable microcosm of our so-

ciety, reflecting all the changes and pressures of modern life."

Representing Hollywood's old guard in purchasing letters were former cowboy star Gene Autry, owner of the California Angels and Hollywood's KTLA, the first commercial TV station in Los Angeles, who purchased the second L. "I came here in 1934," Autry said, "and the sign has more or less been a trademark, like Pepsi or Coca-Cola, to Hollywood. It reminds us of the glamour days, the golden era of Hollywood."

Longtime Hollywood supporters, singer Andy Williams and Blue Book publisher Les Kelley, donated the W and the first L.

Among the other donors were newer names to Hollywood: Warner Brothers Records, the second O; Terrence Donnelly, publisher of Meredith Newspapers, among their chain the *Hollywood Independent*, the H; Giovanni Mazza, Italian movie

The new sign was unveiled to the public on November 11, 1978. Many celebrities worked at making the new sign a reality, but the first breakthrough came when rock star Alice Cooper gave $27,700 for the last "O" in memory of the late Groucho Marx.

producer, the first O; Dennis Lidtke, owner of Gribbitt!, a Hollywood graphics company, the D.

Lidtke, although he was born and raised in Hollywood, is somewhat of a newcomer to prominence in the city and is committed to rechanneling Hollywood's direction. "I am more interested in the restoration of Hollywood," he said before the new sign's unveiling on November 14, 1978, the night Hollywood celebrated its seventy-fifth anniversary with a Diamond Jubilee party. The coming-out party for the HOLLYWOOD sign, held in a driving rainstorm that night, was televised coast-to-coast.

"The sign," Dennis Lidtke said, "is the hook we needed to hang the restoration of Hollywood on."

New Reflections

In September 1978, Dennis and Beverly Lidtke purchased the former El Capitan Theatre on Vine Street and announced plans for the development of a multimillion-dollar entertainment and production center. Still known as the Palace, the complex is an unequaled state-of-the-art disco theater, with the latest in sound and laser technology. In addition, live concerts and plays will be performed in the newly refurbished historic theater. By day the Palace is transformed into a full-service film and video production complex geared to the needs of the motion picture, television, recording and advertising industries. Facilities like this help Hollywood remain the entertainment capital of the world.

Owner of several Hollywood companies—all related ninety-five-percent to the entertainment industry, mostly recording—Lidtke is also involved in new commitments to put together a Hollywood museum.

"I have worked, lived, and played in Hollywood all my life," the forty-four-year-old business executive said. "I want to see Hollywood come back. You look at the names of the stars on Hollywood Boulevard. They've been walked over for years and they haven't lost their glitter. All we need to do is clean up the sidewalk around them."

By late 1978 and through 1979, Hollywood's cleanup and rejuvenation came into its own. "The turnaround has occurred," said Jack Foreman, now the chairman of the newly created Hollywood Historic Trust. "There is a great spirit in the community that wasn't there before. And as time goes on, its momentum will increase. It's been a long pull, and in the next five years you'll see some drastic changes."

Changes in Hollywood in the past two years have already been phenomenal. Buoyed by a $90 million U.S. Department of Housing and Urban Development grant designated for rundown neighborhoods, much revitalization is underway. The first area to be rehabilitated is bounded by Sunset on the north, Melrose on the south, Seward west, and the Hollywood Freeway on the east. It is the largest grant of its kind allocated to one community.

City funds, low-interst loans, and private contributions will add to the reconstruction in other areas. Already twenty shops on Hollywood Boulevard have signed and begun restoration of their storefronts, according to Mike Sims.

Sound stages and facilities are in such great demand that they cannot be renovated fast enough. And the movie industry is alive and well in Hollywood. Its first studio, Paramount, set an all-time sales record in 1978, while the total film industry grossed $3.8 billion, and the recording industry $4 billion.

The entertainment industry," says Sims, "is beginning to realize that the mythical Hollywood and the real Hollywood are one and the same. Hollywood is finally beginning to realize what it has ignored for all these years, for whatever reason."

Soon, Sims hopes, Hollywood will have more to offer its tourists, now estimated to be converging on the city at a rate of 3 to 4.5 million each year. Of the 8.5 million visitors who came to Southern California in 1978, Hollywood was their second preferred destination, outdistanced slightly by Disneyland. One-half of those visitors are from foreign countries, probably the highest number from Japan.

The Hollywood Historic Trust committee has already started to implement some of its plans. Student tour guides, ages eighteen to twenty-four, began directing and advising tourists on Hollywood Boulevard in mid-August, passing out literature to assist them.

The trust also plans "window museums" in many of the shops along the Walk of Fame route, and hopes, by 1980-81 to erect information kiosks at historic sites in the city.

Perhaps the biggest news of all for historic Hollywood is the phased five-year development of a museum. There have been plans before that have gone awry, but this one seems to be taking shape.

There is a tentative location on Vine Street for the museum to get started.

"Paramount is giving us the old barn originally used by DeMille to make *The Squaw Man,* said Sims. "It was moved to their lot in 1926 from its original location at Selma and Vine."

The 4,500 square-foot barn is a state historic monument, but has never been available for the public to visit. Paramount is restoring the exterior; the Chamber of Commerce, though the Historic Trust committee, will be responsible for redoing the interior. Plans at this time are to place the historic building on a site [now occupied by a city parking lot] next to the Huntington Hartford Theatre, across from the newly refurbished Hollywood Brown Derby. "It is so small, it will only take up about twenty parking spaces," said Sims. "But the best thing is that people will be able to see it, tour it."

Construction of garden-office complexes, small shopping centers, rehabilitation of Hollywood Boulevard's many movie theaters are underway or already completed.

Plans are being developed for a major hotel and convention center to be built; the Hotel Roosevelt, the grande dame of Hollywood hotels when it was built fifty-seven years ago, has new owners and is being refurbished after years of decline.

The Chinese Theatre, owned by Mann Theaters Corp., opened two more houses, Chinese II and III, while Pacific Theaters finished a $1 million rehabilitation of its theater at Hollywood Boulevard and Wilcox Avenue. One of the most extensive restoration and renovation programs in Hollywood today is underway at the former Hollywood Athletic Club. The building's new owner, Gary Berwin, is transforming the historic site into an entertainment complex, which will include such features as recording studios, screening rooms, theater, business offices, restaurant, and a mini hotel with thirty luxury suites. Doors to the new complex are expected to be opened in early 1980, giving rebirth to one of Hollywood's most prestigious buildings.

After officiating at the opening of a new Hollywood park on Franklin and Sycamore, donated by retired tax attorney and industrialist Benjamin B. Smith, Mayor Bradley told listeners, "Hollywood today is enjoying a new vitality, a new spirit of optimism. Hollywood has known the glory days of splendor, but it also has seen recently gloomy days resulting from physical deterioration. All of that is changing."

Commercial office space, according to Hollywood Chamber statistics, is almost 100 percent rented, the rent having risen recently from $1 to $1.25 per square foot, comparable to rents in West Los Angeles.

The housing and real estate boom that hit Los Angeles County and outlying areas beginning in 1975 came to Hollywood a little late, probably because of its deteriorated reputation in the early part of this decade. By 1977, though, Hollywood residences had been rediscovered. Newcomers found that it is one of Los Angeles' most centrally located cities [ten minutes from downtown], and that its hillside areas are semirural in setting.

From the 1940s to the past two years, however, real estate in Hollywood remained stagnant, even declined in some cases. One property owner, for instance, bought a building on Hollywood Boulevard in 1938 for $225,000. He sold it in November 1975 for $25,000 less than he paid for it.

Values in the Hollywood Hills were the first to skyrocket. "You must remember, there are two Hollywoods here," says broker Vance Otis, who has been in the real estate business in Hollywood since 1959. "The flatlands and the hills. The flatlands need major progress and upgrading in physical appearance in many areas. Some areas are quite nice, but others have been so neglected that they should be condemned by city building and safety people or by the fire department."

Yet, according to Otis, even in the flatlands of Hollywood it is hard to find a home for less than $80,000 to $100,000. People are finding it easy to get to and from Hollywood, and it is the only place, outside of Westwood, that has any significant nightlife.

"The word is out," Otis said. "Brokers are moving east from Beverly Hills to Hollywood. It is the last area in Los Angeles to catch on. The best place right now in all the county to make investments."

A home in the Beachwood Canyon area that sold for $40,000 in the early Seventies, was valued at $200,000 in 1979. One house on Belden Drive recently sold for $399,000; it was bought in the mid-Seventies for $50,000.

Hollywood also entered the condominium market in the late 1970s, several years behind many other Los Angeles communities. It won't take long to catch up. By early 1979, several large apartment buildings, among them the Hollywood Versaille, at Hollywood and La Brea, and the Los Feliz Towers had converted to condos.

As it modifies in physical composition, Hollywood is also changing in ethnic makeup. Its population, about 200,000, is fifty-two percent minority peoples and forty-eight percent Anglo [in 1975, the city was still over fifty percent in Anglo residents].

"Hollywood is becoming the Ellis Island of the West Coast," Mike Sims says. "Because Hollywood is probably the only English word many of the foreign-borns know when they get to Los Angeles. So they come here."

Spanish-speaking peoples make up twenty-seven percent of Hollywood's ethnic mix today; Asians, seventeen percent, black, six percent. A large and still growing Armenian population has built up in the eastern sector of the city. Five years ago, there were 5,000 Armenians; today, somewhere around 35,000.

Much foreign money is also being invested in Hollywood these days, among the largest groups are the Asians, Vietnamese, Korean, Japanese, Chinese, and Thais, who are purchasing income property such as apartment buildings and offices, and opening restaurants throughout the area.

Students at LeConte Junior High School speak thirty-eight different languages and parent notices are sent home in English, Spanish, Armenian, and Thai. At Hollywood High, the student body, which has experienced a ninety-five percent turnover in two years, is made up of about fifty-three percent minority students. They speak fifty-two languages.

Hollywood always has had a large transient population, due mostly to the fact that it is easily accessible to other parts of the Los Angeles area, has many bus lines, and has relatively low rents. The senior citizens have grown in numbers, too, and now make up one-third of Hollywood's resident community. The city is the second largest senior citizens area related to ratio of population outside of Miami, Florida, a traditional center for retirees.

Because of the influx of foreign-borns and seniors, Hollywood's social service programs are being studied by community and civic groups. They, too, will become part of the changing and revamping of the city.

Approaching Light

"At this point, no city is changing as fast as Hollywood," says Mike Sims. "We have commitments from every government level, from local to the White House. It used to be hard to get anyone to commit to anything; now everyone will. We've come such a long way in the past three years. It appears that the Eighties will be our light at the end of the tunnel."

And there is light—the brightest in decades. Visitors who tour our city in more than 125 tour buses each day are beginning to get a different view of Hollywood. They're finding a new Hollywood with the old, a building and rebuilding, a refurbishing in keeping with its historical reality and image. At this writing, the Hollywood Brown Derby has completed its remodeling and refurbishing; the Hollywood Roosevelt Hotel is in the midst of extensive remodeling; the former Hollywood Athletic Club's exterior has been beautifully restored, and its interior renovation continues; the building's new owner, Gary Berwin,is to be congratulated for restoring the exterior to its former beauty, rather than remodeling it.

Nowhere is the community's revitalization spirit more evident than on Hollywood Boulevard. Small shops like The Posh and Demain are shining examples that preservation can work—as is David Lee's Young China Restaurant, which has been beautifuly restored. Other shop owners and entrepreneurs have joined the revitalization ranks, and their concern and efforts will come to fruition soon. Frederick Mellinger, owner of the world-famous Frederick's of Hollywood, has plans on the drawing board for a nearly quarter-million-dollar renovation of his Hollywood Boulevard headquarters.

Those of us who live and work here are encouraged by the renewed community interest and concern and spirit. In a sense, it's a search for and an examination of communal roots. And it may well have begun with the drive to save the Hollywood sign. There are those in the city who thought Mike Sims was being overly dramatic when he said publicly that if we can't save the sign, we can't save Hollywood. The fact is, Sims knew that the sign was something more than concrete and steel pipe and sheet metal. Regardless of the purpose for its original, utilitarian construction, the sign had become a symbol: literally, of the city's roots, of its expansion and development; figuratively, of the image of Hollywood that is renewed whenever and wherever a motion picture projector is switched on.

For the past two decades, Hollywood's atmosphere has been clouded by the extremes of indifference and cynicism, a defense, perhaps, born of the anguish and frustration at what seemed the inevitability of the city's dark destiny. But there is light now. What is most heartening about the renewed interest, concern, and spirit is that it rekindles pride. And we have much to be proud of.

Index